THE CROSS AND THE GUN

A Gift From
New Life City Church
(Formerly New Life Fellowship)
Sundays 11am & 6.45pm

The Cross and the Gun

JACK MCKEE

THANKFUL BOOKS

First published 2004

Published by Thankful Books
70 Milton Road,
Eastbourne,
East Sussex,
BN21 1SS

ISBN 1 905084 00 5

Book design and production for the publisher by
Bookprint Creative Services, P.O. Box 827, BN21 3YJ, England.
Printed in Great Britain.

DEDICATION

This book is dedicated to all who serve God faithfully in Northern Ireland and in other areas of conflict throughout the world; to those who have chosen the cross over the gun and have not confused or corrupted the former with the latter.

'The weapons we fight with are not the
weapons of the world.'
(2 Cor 10:4)

'For our struggle is not against flesh
and blood, but against the rulers, against
the authorities, against the powers of this dark
world and against the spiritual forces of evil
in the heavenly realms.'
(Eph 6:12)

CONTENTS

FOREWORD

Jack McKee knows about danger. He knows about risk and fear, about self-preservation and self-sacrifice. We all like to talk about how life is a battle, but most of us live on the peripheries of the battleground. Jack lives on the front lines. On purpose.

Jack is an amazing man who has performed phenomenally bold feats for the gospel. But he isn't a thrill seeker. He's a God seeker. He isn't trying to be a hero, but by doing exactly what God has called him to do he has become one of our living heroes.

As you read this book you'll become intimately familiar with Jack's passion. He holds nothing back, and his candor results in an enticing and challenging reading experience. Actually, it's more like a praying experience, because Jack's stories will drive you to your knees. In this era where violence is so much a part of both current events and popular culture, where murder and destruction are ubiquitous, Jack's life and teaching serves as a reminder that the good news of Jesus is ubiquitous, too, because God has called His people to proclaim that good news anywhere and everywhere.

Jack also reminds us that many Christians past and present have confused hate and love. When the gospel becomes part of a political program or ethnic movement, it can be completely subsumed. The good news can be transformed into bad news very quickly, as the events in Northern Ireland and elsewhere have shown us. But it is into situations like those that people like Jack are called, people who step into darkness and proclaim the light.

If, like me, you are an American, it might be difficult to feel the urgency of Jack's message. He lives in a place where the call to lift the cross above the gun is an extreme call indeed, one fraught with risk. Every week or so, Jack sends an email update to many of us detailing the latest violence at the hands of terror-ists. These emails are filled with bomb explosions, assassinations, and people fleeing for their lives. Jack describes a daily war zone and his church's brave efforts to remain in that zone in order to proclaim the true peace available in the gospel.

He is living a phenomenal life, and while our problems are very tame by comparison, there are parallel circumstances on these shores. As president of the National Association of Evangelicals in the United States, I fellowship with a wide array of Christians with differing views on theology and politics, and often I have to navigate in the middle of intense disagreements. Sometimes, factions are well defined, with vivid lines drawn in the sand and threats of separation and exclusion come from both sides. But these factions do not escalate into the kinds of violence we see in Northern Ireland. These divisions, though, do hamper the spread of the gospel. We do not always have to proclaim the cross above the gun, but we do have to proclaim it above other kinds of ideological and spiritual violence that can have dramatic eternal effects.

In sum, I believe Jack's message is essential for all of us. It's about being a peacemaker. It's about developing the wisdom to know that you can respect the differences of others while still strongly maintaining and professing your core convictions. It's about being like Christ, and finding the courage to proclaim peace and love no matter the consequences.

Ted Haggard
Colorado Springs 2004

ACKNOWLEDGEMENTS

I wish to thank all at New Life Fellowship, Shankill Road, Belfast, for their ongoing love, support and understanding as I have sought to fulfil my role as Senior Pastor in a way that is far removed from many of the traditional expectations. Also for their love and support shown to Kathleen and our family, but more so for their love and faithfulness to the One who has called us out of darkness and into His marvellous light. For it is only as we serve Christ together, by serving one another in the unity of the Spirit, that the vision given by God can be fully realized.

To all our friends and partners, who have prayed for us and have supported us during some very difficult and challenging times. The walk of faith may feel somewhat lonesome at times, but it is never entirely lonely. Not while others stand with us in prayer and strengthen us with their words of encouragement. For the successes and achievements that are the legacies of any walk of faith are only made possible by the faithful companionship of those who stand, walk and pray in the bond of Christian love and fellowship.

As Paul said to the Philippians, 'I thank my God every time I

13

remember you . . . [and for] your partnership [fellowship] in the gospel from the first day until now' (Phil 1:3–4). Notwithstanding the work of the Holy Spirit, the success of Paul's ministry was on the back of others who were faithful. I have never known a successful pastor who did not have faithful people in the local church and further afield where necessary.

I thank God also for those who have faithfully stood by me throughout my years of ministry, and especially my wife Kathleen, who has loved and partnered me irrespective of what she, or even I, has sometimes thought of the ministry. And of course my thanks to God, who is always faithful.

For this reason I would like to thank, not only those closer to home, but my many friends in the USA and pastors who have opened their platforms to me. A special thanks to Pastor Ted Haggard for being such an inspiration to the Body of Christ and to me personally and for his willingness to write the foreword for this book. I count it an honour that he should permit his name to be identified with this book and with me personally.

ABOUT THE AUTHOR

Pastor Jack McKee has become somewhat of an enigma to many of his contemporaries, both within the church and within the community he seeks to serve and reach with the gospel of Jesus Christ. Leaving military service in Northern Ireland, where he had served as a member of the Ulster Defence Regiment (UDR) for five years, and having avoided death several times while some of his friends and comrades had tragically been murdered by terrorists, he chose to give up the gun for the greater cause of taking up the cross.

In 1977 he left Northern Ireland to study at the Elim Bible College in England. There he remained and prepared himself for the Elim ministry until 1979, when he graduated and was accepted as a probationary minister. He was finally ordained as an Elim minister in 1982. Jack had attended Bible college with the belief that God was calling him into a ministry that would take him beyond the norm, and would enable him to reach people within his own nation and within the streets of his home community – the notorious Shankill Road.

A more detailed account of his dramatic story of life and

ministry in strife-torn Northern Ireland has been documented in his first book, *Through Terror and Adversity*, published by Alpha Publications and distributed by Kingsway Publications, Eason's and World Books. This can also be ordered on the New Life Ministries website at www.newlifeministriesireland.co.uk

However, in this his second book, Pastor Jack writes about his amazing journey in following through the commitment he made as a Shankill Road teenager to Jesus Christ; a journey that has not only taken him across the world, but more specifically from the streets of Belfast to a Bible college in the south of England and eventually back again to Belfast, where his ministry has taken a leap beyond the norm.

In this book you will read how he purchased a cinema for the purpose of reaching young people in the disadvantaged areas of inner-city Belfast. You will read of his walk through the centre of his own community while carrying a cross during a bloody feud between the UVF and the UDA/UFF Loyalist paramilitaries, when many lost their lives and many more were seriously wounded. You will also read of his incredible and daring 40-Day Cross Walk through the divided and warring communities of the Catholic Falls Road and the neighbouring Protestant Shankill Road in west Belfast.

Finally, you will read of his congregation's courageous faith response to a bloody and deadly feud within the ranks of the UDA/UFF that seriously affected the Lower Shankill, and more specifically the surrounding streets where his church, New Life Fellowship, is located and where many of the families that attend his church actually live.

Chapter One

THE CHOICE IS REAL

Ruth was a member of a wealthy and influential Muslim family living in Egypt. As a young woman she became dissatisfied with life. Believing she would find fulfilment in marriage, she eventually married a fellow Muslim, as is the custom of Islam. However, her new husband soon began to abuse her and continued to do so until he finally deserted her, leaving her with a one-year-old son. Beyond the breakdown of her marriage Ruth continued with her search, as she said herself, 'Trying to find true peace'. She tells of how her search finally came to an end, but only after she had committed her life to Christ while 'secretly' attending a Christian church.

Afraid to tell her Muslim family, Ruth continued to secretly attend church, but soon her family noticed a change. She had become quiet and softly spoken. They thought she might be taking drugs, so they hired two men to follow her. It was then they discovered she had been attending church and had in fact become a Christian. From here on, life would never be the same for Ruth and her young son.

She was locked up in her own room and this became her

prison and torture chamber for the next six weeks, but in the midst of the beatings and persecution, she experienced the reality of the presence of Christ. Again in her own words Ruth said, 'My Jesus never left me.' She went on to say, 'They beat me with no mercy, called me all kinds of nasty names, spat on me, took away everything I owned but my soul, and stopped serving me food. As they were getting ready to kill me, this verse came to me: 'Behold I send you out as sheep in the midst of wolves. Therefore be wise as serpents and harmless as doves'.

Like many others who have been persecuted for their faith in Christ, Ruth continued to hold on to God, who saw her tears and heard her prayers. She goes on to say, 'Miraculously, I got out of my prison. When I showed them anger, became violent and used a loud voice again (my old nature), I started to gain their trust back. Bit by bit they allowed me to get out of the room that had become my prison, and eventually out of the house and into the street again. The first thing I did was to get hold of the pastor of the church I had secretly attended. He advised me to get out of the country immediately.'

Ruth finally managed, again through miraculous interventions, to make it to the USA, where she and her young son have received all the necessary help to settle and adjust to their new life and their newfound freedom. Her family continues to search for her. Sadly the consequence of being found by them would not be a loving reunion, but could be tragic in the extreme.

Her decision to take up the cross and follow Christ became her death warrant in Islam, even within her own family. She did not know that her conversion to Christianity would place her life between the cross and the gun. Yet she is nonetheless determined to follow her convictions by continuing to lift the cross above the gun within her own life and testimony.

Extreme fundamentalism

Historically, when religion takes the place of a genuine personal relationship with God, and when the defence or the promotion of religion is perceived to be the goal, the door to extreme fundamentalism and religious narrow-mindedness opens up and becomes almost impossible to close. The objective for those who hold extreme fundamentalist opinions is often expressed in their desire to maintain and promote their own brand of religion by whatever means. Even if that involves the promotion of bloody violence where the murder of innocent men, women and children becomes justifiable in their own twisted perception of truth and reality, and where the employment of firearms becomes a legitimate means of imposing or defending a religious position, and where the Bible, the Koran and their counterparts in other religions become nothing more than textbooks or religious war manuals.

This has often been the case where certain groups or sects within the various world faiths regularly use violence against those of other religions or belief systems. For example, extreme right-wing Hindus in India have been savagely massacring Christians and Muslims for decades. Reports of such savagery being meted out in various parts of India, particularly in the north, are frequent and many. In one such situation a Christian missionary and his two young sons were barricaded inside their car by Hindu extremists, who then proceeded to set the car on fire. Ignoring the screams coming from within the car, the attackers looked on while the father and his two young sons were burned alive.

In much the same way extreme right-wing Muslims across the world have been guilty of some of the most grotesque murders against Hindus, Jews and Christians. I have met with several people, besides Ruth mentioned above, who by their own choice converted from Islam to Christianity, but were put under a sentence of death by their 'birth religion' for making such a choice. Like Ruth, they had no alternative but to leave their homeland and flee to the USA where they received the necessary help and where they finally became safe, or I should say 'safer'? The fact is the threat against them did not end with their arrival and settlement in the New World, but rather some have been followed and several attempts have been made on their lives.

I remember meeting an elderly woman in a church outside Washington DC. She explained to me that a number of years ago she had been rejected by her neighbours and family and that finally she had to flee from Iran as a result of her commitment to Christ. Later her son also converted from Islam to Christianity, but he too had to flee to the USA. However, he was followed by another member of his family, who finally caught up with him in Virginia. He stabbed the son several times, but thankfully he survived.

Such bizarre attitudes were more publicly evident recently during the war against Saddam Hussein, when a number of extreme right-wing Muslim clerics, in various parts of the Middle East, stood on mosque platforms with the Koran in one hand and a Kalashnikov in the other. Waving both in the air they called upon their listeners to rise up and inflict death on Christians and Jews wherever they could be found.

As the spread of Islam historically owed much of its success to the wielding of the sword, so its maintenance and furtherance, in the minds and actions of such narrow-minded extremists, seems more dependent today upon the use of the sword and the gun than it does upon the power of the word, be it spoken or written.

When people resort to violence for the purpose of imposing their opinions on others, be they government, terrorists or religious extremists, they are admitting to the impotency of their words and their inability to communicate and articulate their case. Such people could not win an argument, and should not be permitted to win 'the war'.

Remember the Crusades

Ah, but for those of us who claim to be Christian, let's pause and reflect for a moment. For it is not enough that we point the Pharisaic finger at others. We must also acknowledge there are those times, past and present, when what is loosely called Christianity presents the same confused and corrupted message, where the cross and the gun have become bizarre bed-partners. This is no more clearly seen than in the Crusades of the eleventh to the fifteenth century.

Pope Urban II instigated the first of the Crusades when he delivered a famous sermon in November 1095 at the Council of Clermont. In it he called upon 'Christians' to unite and to recapture the city of Jerusalem from Muslims. As Mohammed had resorted to violence to impose the spread of Islam, Pope Urban II was likewise willing to resort to the use of bloody violence in his attempt to put down the rise and spread of Islam. His spiritual and religious objective was to reunite the Christian church that was divided between the Latin church and the Greek church, while his territorial Crusade was to retake the Holy City, which at that time was under Muslim control.

Tragically, those involved in this Crusade wreaked havoc and destruction across Europe as they made their way to Jerusalem. Left in their wake were the bodies of murdered Jews and the bloodied wounded who survived to tell the tale of the 'Christian' knights who carried the cross with one hand and wielded the sword with the other. This was followed by their savage and merciless assaults on Muslims when they finally arrived in Jerusalem.

It seems that those who participated in this Crusade had been promised eternal salvation as a reward for their endeavours, yet it also seems that many of them had their sights set on something more earthly and much more immediate and tangible. For most were motivated by their mercenary and selfish aspirations and looked no further than the laying hold of their own piece of the Holy Land. This was something that many of them succeeded in achieving by hacking to death all and any who stood in their way. And they did so with the blessing of 'the church'.

Further Crusades were to follow right through to the fifteenth century during which time cross-carrying, sword-wielding knights traversed land and sea to the Middle East, pillaging, raping and murdering at every opportunity. These were sadly and unfortunately referred to as 'the Christian Crusades'. The unfortunate victims would hear the sound of the approaching marauders, and often the last their eyes would see, before their untimely and bloody deaths, were the white tunics with the emblem of the cross emblazoned boldly upon the chest.

The cross was held aloft in one hand for their victims to see, as if it were the cross that gave the Crusaders the authority to do what they were about to do, and with such belief they proceeded with their dastardly murderous deeds. With the cross in one hand and a sword in the other they would proceed to rape and massacre Jews and Arabs alike. They falsely assumed they were doing God a favour by killing those they self-righteously deemed to be savages. But these Crusaders were the savages.

Some have sought to justify the Crusades by declaring they were a necessary response to the violent spread of Islam across the Middle East. Now there is no getting away from the fact that Islam, as reflected by history, rapidly spread across the world, not by persuasive words, but by the sword. The advancing armies of Mohammed presented people with only one option, which was 'convert to Islam or die'. Tragically many Christians and Jews who refused to accept Allah as God and Mohammed as his prophet were put to the sword.

Yet, in spite of all attempts to explain their actions, it is my opinion that the Crusades can never be justified. Two wrongs cannot make a right, even if we do dress it in religious attire and overshadow it with a cross. The Crusades were to present a corrupt form of Christianity where the savages were those who carried a cross and wielded a sword. Their actions deserved more to be called insanity rather than Christianity.

However, such corruption of the cross has not been confined to the distant past or even to the Middle East. For even in our postmodern world while some have passionately and courageously lifted the cross as a symbol of sacrifice and love, others have used and abused it as a symbol of hatred and division. Such abuse has not only been evident across Europe and in much of the old world, but in more recent years it has stretched across the Atlantic to the New World. The Founding Fathers of the USA did a great thing. They established one nation under God in the hope that all who lived within its borders would be equal and free. We are therefore mindful of and pay tribute to those, past and present, who remain faithful to the cross and to its core values of love, forgiveness and reconciliation. Yet even in this postmodern world, not all who lift up the cross do so with a sense of honour and respect or with any thought of love for the whosoever.

The broken cross

During the twentieth century, the world witnessed the emergence of one Adolf Hitler and his Nazi Party. It has been said that Hitler claimed to be a Christian. His emblem, and that of his notorious Nazi Party, was the swastika, which was nothing more than a broken cross. This corrupted form of the cross was perhaps a true representation of his corrupt beliefs and his fraudulent ideologies. His murderous warmongering across Europe was carried out against Jews and other minorities, including those with disabilities, and was done so, as perceived by many, with a cross in one hand and a gun in the other.

However, Hitler was not the first person, nor was he the last, to unite the cross and the gun in an unholy alliance. For example, notwithstanding the Crusades mentioned above, there are those in our postmodern western society who have likewise tainted the cross by pairing it with the gun. Thankfully, they are in the minority by a long shot (excuse the pun!), but they exist nonetheless; whether it's in the so-called Christian country of Ireland or the so-called 'Bible Belt' of the USA, where the Ku Klux Klan (KKK) is an obvious and sad example of this.

I remember speaking in a church in a southern US state, and while chatting to the pastor afterwards he confided in me that a number of local pastors had got together to pray for their city on a regular basis. He shared with me that one of the pastors had been threatened by one of his own church board members. The pastor was told he would be shot if he continued to attend the united prayer meetings. The reason for the threat was that an African American pastor had also been attending those same meetings.

Many innocents have tragically lost their lives under the night-time gaze of the blazing cross and at the hands of those who iron-ically dressed in white robes that sadistically symbolized purity. Their white robes and over-sized hoods may have covered their faces, but they could never cover the blackness in their hearts. They would ride around on horseback or drive around in beat-up trucks, and would often do so under the cover of darkness. They loved darkness rather than light because their deeds were evil. They held a cross in one hand while they held a gun in the other, and like ravenous wolves they would seek out their unsus-pecting prey. You see, their intention was not to lift up the cross, but to degrade it by misusing and abusing it and by causing it to be a silent witness to their bloody acts of terror.

I suspect that some readers would prefer this subject was ignored, but we must face the truth, or we simply live a lie. We cannot ignore the fact that there are churches in the USA (again just a few, but they are there nonetheless) where photographs of Adolf Hitler 'adorn' the walls. They sing hymns, they pray prayers, they read from the Bible and they preach sermons, but it is all done under the watchful eye of the Führer, yet they claim to be Christians.

One of the most hideous programmes I have watched on tele-vision was on this very subject. The pastor of one of these churches, along with one of his elders, was interviewed during the programme. They spoke of their hatred for Jews and for African Americans (although they used their own racist terminol-ogy). They sought to explain their twisted opinion that to kill someone from these and other religious and ethnic backgrounds was not an act of sin, but an act of divine judgement. In their warped minds they sought to rationalize and justify murder, and all in the name of their twisted perception of religion.

It mattered not to them that their talk was focused on hatred and racism, with no mention of the three great Bible themes of love, forgiveness and reconciliation. It mattered not to them that they spoke, albeit metaphorically (yet I wonder), with a cross in one hand and a gun in the other. It mattered not to them because their cross was a corrupted cross that represented the corruption that existed within their own minds and hearts.

However, let me clearly declare that it does matter to the millions of faithful Christians who honourably seek to obey Christ by taking up the cross and following Him. It does matter to the tens of thousands of preachers who faithfully lift up the cross in their discourses week after week. And by the way, let me also clearly declare – it does matter to God!

Chapter Two

FOR GOD AND ULSTER

It was a cold December Saturday morning. The Maze prison in Northern Ireland was quiet after the Christmas festivities. However, the morning solitude was short lived when Billy Wright died in a hail of bullets in mysterious and questionable circumstances. He had climbed into the back of a prison van in the heart of one of the most secure prisons in Europe, when two armed men suddenly appeared at the back of the van and gunned him down without mercy.

Although he was a Protestant brought up in the notorious South Armagh area of Northern Ireland, Billy Wright had nonetheless been open to understanding Irish history and to developing friendly relationships with the Catholic community. Tragically though, for him and for his victims, this was to radically change. He was only 15 years old when ten Protestant workmen were taken from a minibus and gunned down in cold blood. He later stated, 'I realized that they were massacred because of what I was – a Protestant.' This soon resulted in Billy Wright joining the youth wing of the UVF. When asked why he said, 'I felt it was my duty to defend my people.' This was a clear decision on his part to take up the gun and to become involved in a life dominated by paramilitary activity.

He soon found himself in prison for the first time, but it was then that Billy Wright was confronted with a new challenge: the challenge to give up the gun and take up the cross. He responded to this by making a commitment to follow Christ, and did so for several years even after he had been released from prison. However, pressures mounted and Billy Wright succumbed again to the lure of paramilitary activity, believing it was the only way to defend Northern Ireland from the threat of a United Ireland and to defend the Protestant community from the threat of Republican violence.

He was finally shot dead by members of the Irish National Liberation Army (INLA) on Saturday morning, 27th December 1997. The assassins, who were themselves serving prison sentences for murder, managed to breach stringent prison security without detection. This has led to accusations of a conspiracy and to an official enquiry into the circumstances surrounding this murder. However, for the purpose of this book, the choice between the cross and the gun for Billy Wright was a real one. He chose to live by the latter, fully understanding that those who live by the sword also die by the sword; or in his case, the gun.

Those of us who live in Northern Ireland do not need to look to other histories or to problems in other present day societies before we see such confusion between the cross and the gun. For as a lad at the age of 17, during the tragic events of August 1969, and like many others in Northern Ireland, I too was confronted with such a confused choice: the choice to carry a cross or to carry a gun. Others may not have seen it this way, but I did.

This was at a time when serious street violence had broken out across our nation between Catholics and Protestants. The cities of Londonderry and Belfast had literally been set ablaze with the flames of sectarianism and hatred. There was collateral damage on a scale that had not been witnessed in Belfast since Hitler dropped his bombs on us during the Second World War. Whole communities were displaced from both sides of the sectarian divide. Many were being killed and seriously injured in the daily and nightly street riots and gunfights. The British army was mobilized from mainland UK in the hope that they would restore some kind of normality within Northern Ireland. However, instead of becoming part of the solution, they became part of the problem, losing over 500 of their men and women in the process.

Northern Ireland became the United Kingdom's Vietnam, with one huge difference: Northern Ireland was not foreign territory. Rather, it was, and still is, a full and active member of the United Kingdom, along with Scotland, Wales and England; with the majority of its people being British citizens. During the next 30 years, over 500 British soldiers were to die on this troubled piece of British territory at the hands of those who opposed Northern Ireland's democratically approved membership within the United Kingdom. Some 3,700 people were to die in this tragic conflict where often the cross became associated with the gun, and where religion became entangled in sectarian politics.

The 30 years of political and religious conflict became known as 'the Troubles'. In the early years of this conflict many able-bodied and willing men of all ages, within Catholicism and Protestantism, came onto the streets to defend their respective communities against attacks from 'the other side'. These initially amounted to community vigilante groups. There was an expectation that anyone who was fit and able would do their turn in walking the streets at night while others would try to catch 40 welcome winks. The nights were long and chilling. The smoke-filled mornings were welcomed with a sense of relief, yet with some apprehension as we waited for news from the night before.

As time moved quickly on, these same men, both young and old, who had volunteered as vigilantes, were given the 'opportunity' to join the paramilitary/terrorist organizations that represented their respective communities. Most of those who did so were motivated by the emotion of the moment, but others had thought it through and believed they were justified in joining such organizations. However, they did not foresee the damage these groups would do to Northern Ireland or the control that these organizations would command over their lives and over the life of the community they joined to defend. As Saddam Hussein was being politically conceived in the Middle East with the help of the West, little Saddams were being birthed in communities across Northern Ireland.

A time to choose

Like many of my friends, I was soon facing the same choice to join one of the newly formed paramilitary/terrorist groups within the Shankill community. I remember sitting at home one night, when two men came banging on the front door. They were 'rounding up' all of the able-bodied men in the area, and I was obviously one of them! They instructed me to make my way to a certain place on the Shankill Road, where I would meet with others and receive further instructions. So off I went with a sense of excitement that was balanced with an equal sense of trepidation, but by the time I got to the top end of the Shankill Road there were already several hundred who had gathered for the defence of the community.

I saw men walking around with guns. I saw guns being handed out to those who were 'in the know'. It looked like a scene from a John Wayne movie, only there was no John Wayne. There seemed to be mayhem until someone took control and began to give instructions. We were divided into smaller groups and soon I was standing in the centre of Battenberg Street along with 30 to 40 others. We were lined along the middle of the darkened street, and there standing in front of us was the short stumpy stature of a man who looked and behaved like Captain Mainwaring of Dad's Army (a British sitcom set in World War II).

As he paced up and down in front of us he began to give some kind of military oration, in what appeared to be his 'officerial' maiden speech. It went something like this: 'Well men, you all know why you're here tonight!' However, if the truth was known, the fact was that most of us did not know why we were there at all, although none of us wanted to admit it! With his voice still raised he went on to say, 'You know, men, these are dangerous days for our country, and it is up to people like us to stand up and be counted.' He then sought to encourage us by saying, 'Men, you are not on your own, for in the streets across the Shankill there are many others standing with us.'

As he continued to explain what would be expected of us, I began to sense that most of those who were standing next to me were just as bewildered as I was. And as he neared the end of his 15-minutes-of-fame speech, I became even more bewildered by his summation. His voice suddenly changed from that of a Dad's Army officer in waiting, to one that was more sombre and that added a new dimension to the uneasiness that was already dominating the night.

In fact he seemed to take on the character of Mr Frazer, who was the Scottish undertaker in Dad's Army, for he concluded by saying in a grave and solemn tone, 'Men! Some of you may not make it home tonight, because for some of you this could be your last night on this earth.' But then as if to cheer us he went on to say, 'But I want to tell you that there is a God above who is watching down on you right now.'

Wow! This made me wonder what God must have been thinking of me as I stood there in the dark listening to 'Captain Mainwaring', who proceeded to spend the next couple of minutes encouraging us to reach out to God so that if we did not make it home that night, at least we'd make it to heaven! Then, to top it all, he closed in prayer before sending us off in fear and trembling to patrol the streets in twos (although I think the 40 of us stayed together!) around the streets of the Shankill and to fight almost anything we saw moving.

This was typical of the confusion, even in the minds of those who claimed to be Christians; a confusion that seemed to drag together not only the Bible and the crown within loyal Protestantism, but also the cross and the gun on both sides of the divide. Some were naïve, like our very own 'Captain Mainwaring,' who incidentally never did emerge as a leading terrorist or any other kind of terrorist for that matter. He simply drifted off the 'paramilitary' scene and got on with his Christian life as best he could.

Perhaps he has often looked back to that night, as I have done, and wondered what it was all about. However, not all who united the cross and the gun were as naïve as our well-intentioned but ill-directed, 'Captain Mainwaring'. For the fact is that some were a lot more sinister and a lot more knowledgeable of their actions. They were very much aware of the choices they were making and were deliberately prepared to position the gun alongside the cross as seen by the following examples.

Men of the Kalashnicloth!

There was the self-appointed Protestant pastor who was present at a secret news conference where Protestant terrorists read a statement to the press. On the table in front of the hooded terrorists were a number of guns, hand grenades and an open Bible. The self-appointed pastor apparently prayed and read some verses from the Bible. It was only then that one of the other hooded terrorists proceeded to read a prepared statement that threatened violence against members of the various Republican terrorist organizations and their supporters and also against anyone, even within the Protestant community, who would dare to speak out against them.

Soon after this, a person who had often been referred to by the media as a 'self-appointed pastor' was arrested following the find of several hand grenades. These were found in premises belonging to him, although the premises were vacant when the grenades were discovered. He was soon released without charge, but was later arrested again when a weapon and a primed bomb were discovered in his car during a stop and search operation by police. He is presently serving a 15-year prison sentence. His involvement in terrorism was an embarrassment to all right thinking Christians within the Protestant community and was not representative of its pastors and other ministers.

However, it was not only some within the Protestant community who naïvely or deliberately corrupted the cross with the gun, for equally there were those within the Catholic community who were just as naïve or just as deliberate. It was publicly reported that a certain Catholic priest had allegedly become so involved with the IRA that he rose through the ranks to become a military commander.

It was further alleged that one of the worst atrocities that this priest had orchestrated and overseen was the bombing of a Northern Ireland village in 1972, when a total of nine people became the victims of what the coroner said was 'sheer, unadulterated, cold, calculated, fiendish murder'. All were innocent victims who just happened to be where they were at that particular time of their lives. Some would say that they were at the wrong place at the wrong time, but I am not so sure there is such a place.

Those who died during this bombing spree were Catholics and Protestants, and ranged from children to pensioners. And if the public allegations and reports are correct, then the responsibility for this atrocity lies with an IRA terror group that was commanded by an ill-directed yet cold-hearted serving Catholic priest! However, we might never know the full truth, as the priest in question has since died.

Let me state clearly that neither of the above two men is typical of his respective 'religious' grouping. In fact both of them, as stated above, would be an embarrassment to Protestantism and Catholicism alike. Yet they do unmask the existence and the danger of extremism within religious circles, even within the broad scope of what is called Christianity, where at times the cross is grotesquely partnered with the gun and the bomb.

The reality is that for many living within Northern Ireland, the choice between the cross and the gun has been a real one, although oftentimes a confused or corrupted one. Confused because of the mixed messages at times being sent out by some so-called spiritual leaders, who gave support to the emerging terrorist organizations within their respective communities; corrupted because some saw the gun and the cross as compatible.

While this does not properly reflect the various church denominations in Northern Ireland, nor the views of the vast majority of those who practise their faith within these denominations, the tragedy is that some, albeit a few, within Catholicism and also some within Protestantism have taken their personal beliefs to such an extremity that in their own minds they have managed to justify the corrupt companionship of the cross and the gun.

Others would conveniently declare allegiance to God, but have no respect nor regard for Him. This was epitomized by one such prominent member of an organization in Northern Ireland whose motto is 'For God and Ulster'. He and his young son were walking towards Windsor Park, a local soccer stadium, when someone handed his son a Christian tract. The father immediately took the tract off his son and said, 'You know what to do with that, son, don't you?' He then proceeded to tear it up and throw it to the ground. I have since wondered if perhaps the son might have thought to himself, 'My dad claims that what he does is 'For God and Ulster', but who was that for?'

I might not question this particular person's loyalty to Ulster, although I might do so with others who make such a claim, but I would certainly question his loyalty to God. Loyalty to Ulster or to other places of citizenship might well cause a person to take up the gun to defend its borders and its integrity, but loyalty to God should cause the laying down of the gun and the taking up of the cross. Those who truly have God and Ulster at heart will always seek to defend the integrity of both, although I do understand that some can be easily caught up with the emotion of the moment and can be succoured into making irrational decisions that they withdraw from in the cool light of day and before serious damage is done.

A legitimate use of force

Although I have been a committed Christian for well over 30 years, I am not a pacifist, and I make no apology for it either. I believe the community should take responsibility for its internal safety and security issues, and that the formation of community vigilante groups can be a positive response to civil unrest. However, I also believe that such a response should always be in partnership with the legitimate authorities. I am convinced that while war and violence should only be entered into as a last resort, even when dealing with those who seek to impose their opinions by violence and evil dictatorship, it should nonetheless be a considered and real response to destructive forces and influences.

I fully recognize that as Senior Pastor of New Life Fellowship Church I do not require a firearm to fulfil such a role, although some pastors might well feel they could do with one! However, not all Christians are called to be pastors or missionaries, but rather most are called to live out their Christian commitment in some form of 'regular' employment. Some have chosen to follow a career in law enforcement as police officers, while others have chosen to join the military.

I do not require a firearm while preaching or teaching in church, and neither does the church treasurer while taking up the offering, but those who walk the streets as law enforcement officers or as soldiers, be it in Northern Ireland, New York or Baghdad, often face life-threatening situations, and for this reason they most certainly require the means to defend themselves and to defend the general public.

So believing in a legitimate and disciplined use of force, while others around me were joining paramilitary/terrorist organizations, I made the choice to join the Ulster Defence Regiment (UDR), a properly constituted regiment within the British Army. In recent years, the UDR has had its name changed to the Royal Irish Regiment (RIR) and has served in Iraq as a British regiment, taking control of Umm Qasr and assisting in the taking of Basra. I served as a member of the UDR for five years from 1972 to 1977. During those years I witnessed the deaths of colleagues and friends, while I personally escaped death on numerous occasions. These are documented in more detail in my book *Through Terror and Adversity*.

While serving 'Queen and country' I was a soldier, but a soldier whose first allegiance was to God. I saw no contradiction in this. For example, Joshua was a soldier who fought many battles, but his first allegiance was to God. In fact it was such an allegiance that made him the great soldier and 'master and commander' that he was. Likewise, David was a soldier who served God, but his allegiance to God did not reduce his allegiance to his country. In fact it enhanced his patriotism and was the motivational factor behind him becoming Israel's greatest king, who is still honoured as such today, some 3,000 years after his death. So I saw no contradiction in me being an armed soldier, for legitimate reasons, and at the same time being a Christian committed to the purposes of God. It is possible to serve both God and country, but with the greater allegiance to God.

A man of peace

I fully understand that just as the world has produced men and women who have worked and striven for peace, people like Ghandi and Princess Diana, so Jesus was a man of peace.

However, He was much more than this. In His own words He declared that the peace He gives is 'Not as the world gives'. The peace that He promoted is not as the world understands it. Ghandi saw peace as the laying down of arms and the end of war, while Princess Diana saw peace as achievable through the improvement of circumstances. But the peace that Jesus promoted and also provides has nothing to do with the absence of conflict or war, or even the improvement of physical circumstances and living conditions, much as these might be desired and encouraged. It is a peace in the midst of all circumstances, adverse or otherwise.

Of course Jesus was a peacemaker, but the peace He proclaimed and promoted was first and foremost between God and men: a peace that could not be attained by religious observances, monastic or otherwise, but a peace that could only be experienced by personal relationship with Him. He never condemned war, but this does not mean He approved of it. He never condemned the legitimate law enforcers. He never condemned the military presence that was so evident in His day, particularly with respect to the presence of the Roman Legions that occupied Israel and other surrounding countries. But He did condemn evil and hypocrisy wherever He found it, whether in the higher echelons of the political powers or within the hierarchical ranks of the religious authorities.

The apostle Paul, who many Bible scholars consider to be the greatest of all the apostles and early church theologians, in all his teaching and letter writing, never once condemned the use of force as a legitimate means of maintaining civil law and order. Never once did he condemn or speak against the military presence in Israel or throughout Europe, where he had travelled extensively. In fact, Paul used the military presence as a teaching aid, even as Jesus had done during several teaching sessions.

For example, in chapter 7 of Luke's Gospel, Jesus is approached by a Roman centurion whose servant is dying. When Jesus offered to go with him to his home, the man said, 'Lord, do not trouble yourself, for I am not worthy that you should enter under my roof, but say the word and my servant will be healed.' He went on to say, 'For I also am a man placed in authority, having soldiers under me. And I say to one, 'Go,' and he goes; and to another, 'Come,' and he comes; and to my servant, 'Do this,' and he does it.'

Luke then records that in response to this 'Jesus marvelled', and that He immediately turned to those who followed Him and said, 'I have not found such great faith, not even in Israel.' He did not lecture or condemn the centurion for his career choice, but rather He responded positively to him by healing his servant.

Likewise Paul, in Ephesians chapter 6, uses the uniform and the sword of a soldier to help him teach his lesson on Christian armour and warfare. There he speaks of the belt of truth that holds in place the loose garments that would hinder on the battlefield. He speaks of the breastplate of righteousness and the feet that are properly fitted with the readiness that comes from the gospel of peace. He speaks of the shield of faith that protects against the enemy's flaming arrows and of the helmet that not only protects the head, but also provides salvation; and then he speaks of the sword of the Spirit, which he explains is the word of God.

So for those of us who are committed Christians, when it comes to promoting the gospel we should be doing so through word and deed in the power and anointing of the Holy Spirit. We must always acknowledge that the weapons we fight with are the spiritual weapons of faith, prayer, praise, worship and God's word. This is why Paul said, when writing to the Corinthian church, 'My message and my preaching were not with wise and persuasive words, but with a demonstration of the Spirit's power' (1 Cor 2:4).

Our greatest challenge is not to pick up the gun, but to lift up the cross. The use of the gun, no matter what the circumstances or the perceived legitimacies, is a demonstration of weakness and of failure, whereas the lifting up of the cross, as an emblem of reconciliation and love, is a demonstration of strength and power.

Chapter Three

THE CHRISTIAN RESPONSE TO TERRORISM

The first thing that needs to be understood, not only from a Christian perspective, but also from a basic humanitarian perspective, is that terrorism is not a legitimate use of force, but rather it is a scourge on any society; it is an affliction upon humanity; it is morally wrong. And although it is only one symptom of all that is wrong within our world, it is nonetheless one of the more tragic expressions of iniquitous and criminal behaviour.

Terrorism not only has serious consequences for the unfortunate and oftentimes innocent victims and their families, but also has serious consequences for the terrorists themselves, for their families and for the wider community. It not only diminishes its immediate victims, but it diminishes all of us in that it makes victims of all of us. For example, when the Twin Towers and the Pentagon were attacked on 9/11, and Flight 93 came down in Pennsylvania, some 3,000 people sadly and tragically lost their lives, but while they and their families were the immediate victims, the entire American nation felt victimized and the entire world was diminished. So much so that the world changed that day.

I remember that when the IRA detonated a bomb on the Shankill Road on 23rd October 1993, killing nine innocent people, the entire Shankill community felt a real sense of bereavement. The same could be said of the Lower Ormeau community where Loyalist gunmen shot dead five Catholic men in a bookmaker's in 1992. While the immediate families experienced the greatest loss, whole communities were united in grief and everyone became a victim in one way or another.

A wife might lose a husband at the hands of terrorists, while another wife might lose her husband to the prison system. The same could be said of children, that while some have lost their fathers to terrorism, others have lost their fathers to prison incarceration. Some will spend the rest of their lives visiting the grave of their father, their son or their husband, while others will spend years going back and forth to prison on regular visits.

However, while those who travel back and forth to prison can at least see and touch their loved one and can look forward to being reunited someday, the fact is they are nonetheless victims of the same act of terror that their incarcerated loved one inflicted upon others.

Terrorism is an attack upon all of us, but is also an indictment upon all of us. It makes no difference if it is being carried out in the name of Allah or in the name of God; in the name of the Palestinian cause or in the name of the Israeli cause; in the name of Ireland or in the name of Britain; in the name of Catholicism or in the name of Protestantism; in the name of Republicanism or in the name of Loyalism. Whatever its background or whatever the perceived cause, terrorism is morally wrong. Our first response, therefore, and that of all right thinking people, should be to recognize that terrorism is intrinsically immoral; it is wrong.

Terrorism should be condemned

However, to recognize that something is morally wrong is insufficient if it is followed only by silence, particularly from within the church. It is my firm conviction that the church does not simply possess a mandate to communicate God's love, but that it is also mandated to be an expression of God's abhorrence of evil. The church therefore should not remain silent in its condemnation of terrorism, for the very nature of terrorism is so off beam morally that it not only needs to be condemned, but it should be condemned without qualification.

Failure to be unequivocal in this matter can only mean one of the following: that we have become indifferent to the social evils of our day and are like the proverbial bird that has its head buried in the sand; that we are willing to condone certain actions as long as they fit with our religious or political agenda; that we are prepared to justify terrorism in certain situations; or perhaps that we are fearful of the possible consequences of being outspoken.

There have been many tragedies in Northern Ireland that have made us all victims of terrorism in one form or another. However, it is not just the specific act of terror that should concern us, but we should equally be concerned about our response. For example, in 2002, during the height of serious disturbances in north Belfast, blast bombs and petrol bombs had been thrown and several shots had been fired, and five Protestants had been shot and wounded. But the final response in this saga of violence was from a Loyalist terror group, who sadly took the life of a 17-year-old Catholic lad and then said to the Catholic community, 'We warned you.'

As has always been the case in Northern Ireland, one act of violence led to another, and each in turn being more serious than the one before, leading to the shooting of five men and to the eventual murder of a young man. What probably started with sectarian verbal abuse and the throwing of a single stone, ended in the tragedy of another sectarian and senseless killing.

Immediately following this a Protestant church minister, while doing a television interview, rightly expressed his horror at the above murder, but then he went on to give an explanation as to why this young man had been shot dead. He did so by pointing out that this tragic death was due to the ongoing violence coming from the Catholic community. Now I know he was not condoning the murder of this young man – in fact he was doing the opposite – but there was the perception that by expressing some kind of 'reason' for this murderous act, it could in some way be excused or even justified.

During this same period we were constantly being bombarded by a Catholic priest, via the media, who saw no wrong in the people he represented, but he sought rather to cover their acts of violence with a cloak of respectability by giving some kind of justification to it. The fact is you cannot justify one act of terrorism over another, because one is as reprehensible as the other. Margaret Thatcher, Prime Minister for the United Kingdom of Great Britain and Northern Ireland during the 1980s, rightly said, 'A terrorist is a terrorist is a terrorist.'

Now there is no doubt that we are to live and minister within our respective communities, but this should not blind us to the evil that exists among us while at the same time clearly seeing it on 'the other side'. The Christian response should not include the clergy becoming apologists for the violent, but should be bold enough to the point that we call a spade a spade, even when it is standing in front of us, or perhaps being pointed in our direction in the shape of a gun. Failure to do so corrupts the message and confuses those who are listening to what the respective church leaders are saying.

Terrorists can change

However, while the Christian response should include the willingness to recognize terrorism for what it is and the willingness to condemn it in all its forms, it should also include the recognition that the terrorist can change. Generally speaking, a terrorist is someone who believes strongly in what they are fighting for. They might well be totally wrong, but they are totally committed. They believe strongly enough in what they see as 'the cause' that they are willing to kill and are willing to be killed for it. No matter what their act of terror and no matter who they kill or how many they kill, they believe their cause is just and therefore do not see they are doing wrong. In fact they do not even see themselves as terrorists, but as soldiers. Some within Northern Ireland have expressed regrets for their actions, particularly for the taking of life, but others have made it clear they have no regrets and that given the same set of circumstances they would do it again.

When the IRA announced its ceasefire on 31st August 1994 it made no apology to the victims of its violence; six weeks later the combined Loyalist groups responded by likewise announcing a ceasefire, but they did so with an additional ingredient, for their spokesperson stated the following at a televised press conference: 'In all sincerity, in all sincerity, we offer to the loved ones of all innocent victims abject and true remorse.' One prominent Loyalist spokesperson was later asked the following question relating to the above statement: 'Did he speak for you?' He responded by saying, 'Absolutely, without doubt, without doubt.'

US senator George Mitchell, who chaired the 'Peace Talks' in Northern Ireland, later stated, 'One of the great lessons from this process is the capacity for personal redemption, the ability for [violent] people to accept responsibility, to be punished for it, to accept their punishment and then change.' However, one other prominent Loyalist spokesperson was later asked if he had any regrets concerning two murders for which he had been convicted. He answered by saying, 'No, I have no regrets.'

The apostle Paul tells us that those who do such things are caught up in a web of sin and are in fact blinded by the god of this world, but none more so than the terrorist who cannot, or will not, admit they are doing wrong. Nevertheless, it is possible for their eyes to be opened and for them to come to an understanding of reality. It is possible for their lives and attitudes to change in such a way that rather than take from society, they actually put something back. This is what happened to Paul, who prior to his conversion was a Pharisee to the religious Jews, but to the early Christians he was a terrorist.

Anyone who did not see it Paul's way, when he was a Pharisee, would likely find themselves secured to the whipping post or on the receiving end of the executioners' stones. One such person was Stephen, whose only crime in Paul's eyes was that he proclaimed Jesus of Nazareth to be the Jewish Messiah. Paul, with the Jewish legal system on his side, managed to secure Stephen's death by stoning. He also, as the main witness against Stephen and as was the custom of the day, held the garments of those who carried out the execution.

Paul, however, or Saul of Tarsus as he was known then, was to experience such a change in lifestyle and attitude that he became one of the greatest proponents of the same gospel message that he had violently opposed at that time and for which he had secured the execution of Stephen. The religious system to which Saul of Tarsus belonged had one perception of him, whereas those who were terrorized by him had a very different perception.

In much the same way, a person who plants a bomb and kills innocent people might be nothing more than a terrorist to some, but to others that same person is a freedom fighter or a hero. Someone who straps explosives around his body and walks onto a bus fully loaded with unsuspecting victims might well be the son of a grieving mother back home somewhere, but he is also the faceless agent of terror who takes the lives of innocent sons and daughters and leaves numerous other parents grieving the loss of their children (unless of course they died alongside them in the same barbaric act of terror, which is often the case).

Some people living in Northern Ireland might well consider those who planted the Shankill bomb that killed nine innocent people on 23rd October 1993 as liberators, but to most others they are terrorists. The same could be said of those who planted the Omagh bomb on 15th August 1998 that killed 29 people, and of those who planted the Dublin and Monaghan bombs on 17th May 1974 that killed 33 people. The term 'people' includes whole families, children and babies.

However, the fact is that while they are to be condemned for their acts of violence and terror, they can also be forgiven. Maybe not by the grieving relatives, and maybe not by many within society, but by a God who is the judge of all the earth, and who is not willing that any should perish, but that all should come to repentance and turn away from doing evil. For while the pen is mightier than the sword, the cross is mightier than the gun. And it is through the cross that all may be forgiven, not through expressions of remorse or acts of confession, but through genuine repentance.

Michael Corleone, an Italian American Catholic Mafia boss, while speaking to a Catholic priest in *Godfather III* said, 'What's the point in confessing if I do not repent?' However, the fact is that some do repent, and for them there is forgiveness and there is change. For as Paul said, 'If *anyone* is in Christ, he is a *new* creation; the old has gone, the *new* has come!' (2 Cor 5:17, italics mine).

He fought the cross and the cross won

A leopard might not be able to change its spots, but a terrorist can change his lifestyle. He or she can be turned around for good. Saul of Tarsus was ruthless. He caused much grief and much pain, but his life was changed and he became one of the greatest leaders within the early church. He fought against the cross, but the cross won, and if this could happen in the life of Saul of Tarsus, it can surely happen to anyone.

This also means that if there's hope for the terrorist, there's hope for all of us, for if the worst among us can change then surely the best among us can also change if and when required. I personally have witnessed a number of people involved in terrorist organizations, including some who were actively involved in serious acts of violence, have their lives completely turned around. I have seen them walk away from violence and become positive contributors to the broader community. I have seen those who stole steal no more; I have seen those who kill kill no more. The fact is people can change.

There are some who are known to me personally, who are among those who have chosen to give up the gun and take up the cross. In other words, they have become committed Christians, although not exclusively so, for others have also given up the terrorist lifestyle because they have grown weary, or simply because they have done their bit, or perhaps for some other reason. However, I have also seen first-hand evidence of the fact that those who have been forgiven much also love much.

This does not mean that we should go soft on terrorists, but rather the very opposite. In fact, it is my belief that the Christian church should be giving a lead in taking a public and clear stand against terrorism in all its forms. The church, whatever the religious persuasion, should certainly not be taking sides and should not be seen to be condoning one terrorist organization over another, even though circumstances and location at times make it easier and even prudent to do so.

The cross is not a symbol of terror, but one of love and self-sacrifice, not just on the part of Jesus Christ, but for all who claim to be Christian. It was for this reason that Jesus said, 'Take up [your] cross and follow me' (Mt 16:24). The cross is more a symbol of life than a symbol of death, for Jesus is not calling us to blindly follow Him like lemmings to our death, but to follow Him in life. Some who follow Him might be called upon to die for Him, but all who follow Him are called to live for Him. Jesus said, 'I have come that they [you] might have life, and have it to the full' (Jn 10:10).

The cross is a symbol of death in so far as it represents the death of Christ, the death that He has died for all, and it also represents our death to self, to sin and to the devil. However, beyond the cross there is life, and this is where Jesus wants to get us; that in dying to self we might live unto God. The cross therefore should never be compromised with the gun or with any other weapons of terror and destruction, for these represent death, whereas the cross represents life.

Chapter Four

FAITH IN ACTION

As far as Christianity is concerned, the challenge is not to add guns to faith, but to add legs to faith by taking up the cross and following in the footsteps of Christ. Faith in action is not about guns and violence, but about the cross and reconciliation. It's not about imposing faith with the use of the Armalite or the sword, but about the promotion of faith through word and deed.

Many people living in Northern Ireland claim to have some kind of faith, even among those who have been caught up in the various terrorist organizations. In fact the Protestant terror groups have often claimed that what they do is done 'For God and Ulster' and that they are 'Defenders of the Faith'. One particular terrorist commander at one time said to me, 'Don't get me wrong, Jack. There have been those times when I have prayed and asked God for help.' Another said, 'I think if we were honest, most of us would admit that when our backs are against the wall we pray and make all kinds of promises to God, but only to forget them afterwards.' Well, at the time of writing this book, this person has his back against the wall. I hope he's praying, but that he is also willing to turn from his violent connections and lifestyle. Not just to confess, but to repent.

The confusion here is that when Jesus said, 'Go,' He was not sending His followers out to impose their faith by physical force and violence, but He was commissioning the church to become active in the peaceful promotion of its faith and to disseminate the gospel of peace and love throughout the world by the power and demonstration of the Holy Spirit.

This does not mean that the Christian faith is feeble, for we have seen already it is involved in a battle, but a battle in which the enemy is clearly identified as spiritual rather than physical. The apostle Paul makes it clear that confrontation on a physical level is not the objective of the Christian. On the contrary he says, 'As far as it depends on you, live at peace with everyone' (Rom 12:18).

The problem is that some who claim to be Christian have chosen to add guns to their faith and to promote a bloody message of division instead of promoting reconciliation and unity. Some have even gone as far as to pray over their weapons before using them to kill. This is something we have witnessed in Northern Ireland during the years of 'the Troubles'. However, we must also acknowledge that this is not only something that is practised by certain terrorist organizations in Northern Ireland or by Costa Nostra Mafia bosses who do drugs and commit murder on Saturday and attend church on Sunday, but it is also practised by governments and by legitimate military forces across the world.

Such ritual therefore, as described above, is not unique to Northern Ireland. For example, the same could be said of some far-right white organizations and extreme African American groups within the USA, and also of terrorist Hindu organizations in India, who revere the life of the cow, but have little regard for the lives of fellow humans. Likewise, the same can be said of extreme militant Muslim organizations that promote the sacrifice of young men and women as human bombs on suicide missions in the pursuit of their desire to globalize Islam and to destroy their enemies. The tragedy is that some have so little confidence in the strength of their arguments that they feel the need to resort to violence and intimidation.

During one of my visits to New York, I had a group of young people with me from New Life Fellowship. Pastor Aimee Cortesse, of Crossroads Tabernacle in the Bronx, purchased tickets for us to see some of the shows on Broadway. As some of us stood in Times Square, waiting for other members of our group, we noticed what looked like an open-air service. Knowing we still had some time on our hands I walked across Times Square with one of our young men, Paul McAuley, to check out what we thought was a Christian open-air service!

When we got to the centre of Times Square, we moved towards a makeshift platform that was standing about four feet off the ground. Positioned at each of its four corners was a man dressed like a Ninja fighter. Each one stood with his hands stretched out in front of him holding what looked like some kind of sword in a sheath. At first sight I thought these might have been the local church elders!

Standing on the platform were another three men. The one in the centre held a microphone and was doing most of the talking, while the other two men stood on either side of him. Both of these men were standing behind a lectern with an open Bible on top. From time to time the speaker (the man in the middle) would make reference to a verse from the Bible and would then hold the microphone to the mouth of one of the other two men, who would then proceed to read the verse with some enthusiasm and a dash of amateurish theatrics.

As we continued to stand in the middle of the crowd that had gathered to watch the spectacle unfold before us, it soon dawned on us that we were the only two white skinned people standing there. The more the speaker talked, the more I realized this was not a good situation. We began to feel even more uncomfortable when the speaker lifted a portrait of a 'white Jesus' with 'SATAN' written across his face. He then proceeded to claim that America belonged to the African Americans, and that they (the African Americans) were the true descendants of Abraham.

I began to smile at the very thought of this claim when the speaker suddenly turned his eyes in my direction. He seemed to look straight at me, his eyes looking much like those of the snake in *Jungle Book*. Soon all doubts were gone and I knew he was speaking to me when he began to challenge me with obscenities about the white Americans and about Jesus, the 'white Messiah'.

The situation quickly began to deteriorate, while Paul and I were getting more and more nervous by the second. At one point Paul leaned over and nervously whispered, 'Com' on, Jack. Let's go.' I turned my head to the left and whispered back, James Cagney style through the side of my mouth, 'Wait a few minutes, Paul. Don't let them see you're afraid of them!' But if the truth were known!

However, as I was nervously trying to encourage Paul to stand for a few moments longer, I could feel the closeness of someone standing menacingly next to me. I could almost feel the warmth of his breath on the back of my neck, and it soon became apparent that he was a companion of the 'preacher' on the platform and possibly one of his elders, or should I say 'Ninja bodyguards'? It was then that I leaned over and whispered again to

Paul. Only this time it was more of an Oliver Hardy to Stan Laurel style and said, 'Let's go, Paul, but don't run, just walk!'

Soon we were back with our friends on the other side of Times Square. We were both glad the experience had ended and were quietly thinking to ourselves, 'Those guys didn't know who they were messin' with! They didn't know we were from the Shankill!' However, the sight of a man reading a Bible and preaching while surrounded by Ninja-style bodyguards just didn't look right.

It is my understanding that those who claim to be committed to the Christian faith, as opposed to being committed to religious Protestantism or religious Catholicism, or to any other religion for that matter, should be adding legs to their faith as opposed to guns or Ninja jumpsuits and swords. Christianity is not an 'ism' or a dogma that imposes itself upon people. Nor does it seek to impose burdensome man-made rules and regulations on its adherents. It is a heartfelt desire to know God and to follow His Son, Jesus Christ.

This is clearly expressed in the outworking of a Christ-like lifestyle that seeks to follow the teachings and the examples of Christ, even to the point of being willing to take up the cross in our spiritual pursuit. Never once did Jesus encourage His followers to take up the sword or the gun as they followed Him, but rather to take up the cross as a symbol of self-sacrifice and a life devoted to God.

The journey of real biblical faith is one of personal obedience to the call of God, which is not without its challenges. These challenges are many and varied, as depicted in the amazing story of *The Pilgrim's Progress*; a story that shows Pilgrim's remarkable pursuit to find personal forgiveness and freedom from the burden and bondage of sin. A freedom that he finally found in the cross and in the discovery of God's will for his life. Such freedom is offered to all, but is only found by those who make it to the cross and who surrender all that they have and all that they are to Christ. The evidence of such faith is not in the songs we sing or in the Bible translation we read, but in our attitude to each other and in our attitude to the lost, whoever they are. For sometimes our attitude is like the body of Lazarus after four days in the tomb: 'It stinketh!' (AV).

One small step

The first challenge that usually confronts any person who feels the need to respond to God's call is to simply get up from where they are and to begin to move forward in pursuit of that call. Neil Armstrong, whose family came from Northern Ireland, on setting foot on the moon, uttered those now famous and immortal words, 'One small step for man; one giant leap for mankind.' Yet he could never have taken that small step onto the surface of the moon had he not taken the initial small step towards the craft that would finally take him there.

By the same token, Moses could never have fulfilled God's will and purpose for his life by staying in the backside of the desert. His burning bush experience in Exodus 3 and 4 was not an end in itself, and was certainly not for the purpose of writing the latest worship song or establishing the 'First Church of the Burning Bush' in the desert place. The purpose of such an experience was to propel him forward. The challenge to Moses was not that he would simply believe in God, but that he would add legs to his faith and would step out on a journey of obedience that would take him from the backside of the desert and into the kingdom of the Pharaohs in pursuit of an amazing destiny.

James said, 'Faith by itself, if it is not accompanied by action, is dead' (Jas 2:17). However, if I can be so bold as to say it, faith is not static and is not legless. Faith does not only sink you to your knees, but it puts you on your feet and propels you forward. Faith without legs is motionless and will not take you anywhere, except maybe to church on Sunday! Faith is not passive, but active. It is not just about what you believe, but is more about what you do with what you believe. That's why James also said, 'Show me your faith without deeds, and I will show you my faith by what I do' (Jas 2:18).

Faith is not a dependence in your own ability to manipulate or even intimidate, but is a dependency on God to work things out His way and in His time. King Solomon said, 'He has made everything beautiful in its time' (Ecc 3:11). Faith is not only something you work out with your intellect, if that be possible, but is something you work out in practice. However, faith is not only something you work out, but is also something you walk out in the belief that every place upon which the soles of your feet tread has become your spiritual inheritance and has been given to you by God.

One of the ways we can walk out our faith, as you will see later in this book, is to lift up the cross in the streets of our communities and our cities, as opposed to lifting up weapons of destruction; to lift up the cross as a symbol of love and reconciliation, and as something that is more powerful than the gun. By so doing, we lay claim to those same streets for the kingdom of God. We enter battle in the heavenly realms, confident of victory, and we impact our communities for good. For as God said to Joshua, so He says to us and to this generation, 'I will give you every place where you set your foot, as I promised Moses' (Josh 1:3).

Moreover, Jesus said, 'Go *into* all the world and preach the good news to all creation' (Mk 16:15, italics mine). This demands a response on our part, calling not just for passive assent, but for action. It demands the kind of action that causes us not only to walk but also to go with a sense of destiny, and to do so with the knowledge that Jesus has said, 'But I, when I am lifted up from the earth, will draw all men to myself' (Jn 12:32).

We are not called to a static faith, but to a living faith, a vibrant faith. We are called to live by faith and also to walk by faith. That means doing more than talking the talk; it means walking the walk. It means adding legs to our faith, which consequentially will enable us to do three things: to stand, to walk and to run.

Legs to stand

In his desire to see every generation of Christians properly equipped and prepared to stand in the face of opposition and persecution, the apostle Paul declared, 'Put on the full armour of God, so that when the day of evil comes, you may be able to stand your ground, and after you have done everything, to stand. Stand firm then' (Eph 6:13). If for no other reason, we should put legs on our faith so that we can at least take our stand against the forces of evil that array themselves against us and against our world and our communities. We should be willing to stand at all times and in all situations, and at times to stand with the cross raised high as a sign of our boldness and our determination to stand firm come what may.

Failure to do so will once again result in being burdened by the yoke of slavery from which Christ has set us free. This is why Paul said; 'It is for freedom that Christ has set us free. Stand firm, then, and do not let yourselves be burdened again by a yoke of slavery' (Gal 5:1). Furthermore, failure to stand firm in our faith and in our commitment to Christ and to each other will bring discredit and dishonour to the message of the gospel that we claim to love. It was for this reason that Paul said, 'Conduct yourselves in a manner worthy of the gospel of Christ. Then . . . I will know that you stand firm' (Phil 1:27). People who live in fear and often succumb to weakness will not be drawn to a fear-ridden, spineless, weak-kneed church, but will be attracted to a church that stands firm in the midst of confrontation and persecution.

A church congregation in America had gathered for worship on a Sunday morning, as was its normal practice. Just before the service was due to begin, several men burst into the main sanctuary where the people had gathered. The men were all wearing black facemasks and were armed with guns. They took up different positions around the church, with one of them making his way to the front. Terror had taken hold of those who had gathered for worship as the man who had made his way to the front menacingly took his place on the platform.

Armed and looking dangerous, he addressed the congregation and gave them an ultimatum: leave quickly or remain behind and suffer the consequences. Most of the congregation, gripped with fear or simply the desire for self-preservation, got up and quickly left the building.

Immediately after they had done so, the man on the platform removed his facemask revealing to those who had remained in their seats that he was in fact the pastor of the church. He congratulated those who had stayed behind and then invited them to join with him as he proceeded with the morning service. The other masked men were also members of the church leadership team.

The fact that I mention the above story does not mean I would advocate this method of testing a church's commitment.

However, it does serve to make the point that if such a situation were to arise, not everyone would stand firm. Moreover, we do well to remind ourselves that in reality certain situations actually do arise in various parts of the world where those involved are not play-acting and where the choice to escape death is not even an option. This is confirmed by the following story.

It was Sunday 20th November 1983. The 60-strong congregation of Mountain Lodge Pentecostal Church in the tiny village of Darkley, Northern Ireland, were in their places for the evening service. Three church elders, who were standing at the front door of the little church, had planned to join with the congregation, but only when they were certain that all of their friends and guests had arrived and taken their seats inside the church building.

As the congregation was singing the opening hymn, 'Are you washed in the blood of the Lamb?', and before the elders could take their seats, a car pulled up outside the church. Several men stepped out of the car. They were all armed members of the Irish National Liberation Army (INLA), which is nothing more than a sinister and murderous terrorist organization that with the IRA is opposed to the democracy that exists in Northern Ireland.

While the music was playing and the people were singing, the three church elders were cold-bloodedly gunned down in the entrance hall by these so-called 'Liberation soldiers'. Moments later, not satisfied with the murder of three unarmed and innocent church elders, the terrorists proceeded to rake the church with automatic gunfire, wounding seven more people, including one woman who was shot in the stomach five times. The building where this atrocity had taken place was later lifted and moved to a nearby site. A new church building was erected in its place and was opened in honour of those who were mercilessly gunned down. The guns of terror might well have shed innocent blood once again, but the message of the cross is still being proclaimed.

Legs to walk

In Mark's Gospel, chapter two, it was not enough for the paralytic to have faith and still remain in his bed. He had to activate his faith by getting up from his bed and by actually walking. He was required to put legs on his faith; otherwise he would have remained in his bed of helplessness. Jesus asked the following question, 'Which is easier: to say to the paralytic, "Your sins are forgiven," or to say, "Get up . . . and walk"?' (Mk 2:9). I think we all know the answer to this question!

It is also one thing to say, 'I believe,' and to preach sermons and sing songs expressing such belief, but it is another thing to take a step beyond our sermonizing, our sermon tasting and our singing of songs. It is another thing to add legs to our faith so that we can rise from our beds of indifference and begin to walk as God intended us to walk; to walk in the light as He is in the light; to walk according to His counsel and not according to the counsel of the wicked; to walk by faith and not by sight; to walk through storms and to walk through fire, knowing that every step we take is another step forward, another step of achievement and another step of victory.

In Bunyan's The Pilgrim's Progress, before Pilgrim could find the very thing his heart had been longing for, he first had to rise up from where he was and begin to take the necessary steps that would bring him ever closer to his objective. He would never have known freedom had he not walked from his imprisonment. His overwhelming sense of guilt would never have been eliminated had he not got up and walked the walk that would ultimately get him to the cross. Some things may well come to those who wait, but achievement and victory come only to those who get up and go, and whose faith is active.

When God called Abraham, it was not enough that God had made him several promises concerning his future and that of his descendants, but Abraham needed to rise up and walk the walk that would enable him to take hold of the promises of God. He could not have discovered God's will and purpose for his life by staying where he was. Abraham was very much aware of this, so in response to God's call, he got up from where he was and moved out in pursuit of a new destiny (Heb 11:8).

When James said, 'Abraham believed God, and it was credited to him as righteousness' (Jas 2:23) he was not just referring to what Abraham believed in his heart about God and about His promises, but he was actually referring to what Abraham did because of what he believed. He was referring to the fact that Abraham stepped out, moved forward, believed God for the unforeseen and trusted God with complete and reckless abandonment. Hebrews says, 'He . . . obeyed and went, even though he did not know where he was going' (Heb 11:8).

Similarly, the Children of Israel, who had spent 400 years in Egypt as slaves to Pharaoh and their Egyptian taskmasters, needed to pack up and rise up. This they did, and having done so they stood prepared with staff in hand and shoes on feet, but they then needed to begin their trek across the desert by moving out from where they were. Without doing so, they could never experience freedom; they could never discover what lay beyond the borders of Egypt; they could never taste the grapes and the honey that awaited them in Canaan. It was not enough that they should simply believe the words of Moses and remain in Egypt. But rather they needed not only to believe, but to respond by adding legs to their faith.

This is precisely what they did, for not only did they pack their bags and stand prepared, but when the call went out, they stepped forward and began their walk to freedom. Their walk of faith would be hampered by many obstacles, such as the Red Sea, the wilderness, the River Jordan and walled cities, but it would also take them to their destination and to the ultimate fulfilment of their destiny.

However, the sad reality is that there are many who claim to have faith because of what they believe, but they will never actually go anywhere in God, simply because they are not prepared to rise up, move out and move forward. There are some who claim to have faith, but are not prepared to meet the challenges that true discipleship brings; not prepared to walk the walk of faith; not prepared to cross the Red Seas that rage against them; not prepared to cross the Jordan Rivers and other obstacles that block the way to new and uncharted territory. Rather than grasping hold of new opportunities and believing God for the impossible, they would choose to stay where they are or, in some cases, return from whence they came.

The feeling of hopelessness and helplessness begins to overwhelm as they become convinced that the way ahead is well and truly blocked. They choose to remain in their comfort zone and to hold on to their own securities rather than step out and trust God in the midst of the unknown and for the impossible. In some cases, this places the gun above the cross, because the gun provides a sense of security, whereas the cross exposes vulnerability and presents the greater challenge. Sadly, this is the choice that confronts many in Northern Ireland, as in other parts of the world, and for some the gun becomes the preferred choice.

While speaking with one such person who was spending

several years in prison, I challenged him to examine the choices he had made that finally landed him prison. He responded to me by saying, 'Jack, there is not a waking moment in my life that I do not think of these things.' However, simply thinking about these things, without acting upon them by making the right choices, is not sufficient. There are many who have gone through the process of thinking about their actions, but they have failed to take the necessary steps that would bring about the required and desired change.

However, the same Bible that teaches that nothing is impossible to God also declares, 'Everything is possible for him who believes' (Mk 9:23). It is therefore my firm belief that God will always make a way, even when there seems to be no way, and that for every Red Sea, there is God's provision of a clear and dry passage that leads safely from the banks of despair and deficiency to the unfolding blessings and provisions of God.

It is God's desire that we all experience His blessings and provisions. His call, therefore, goes out to all of us that we enter into those blessings and into all that He has purposed and planned for us. You see, whenever God calls you, He does so because He wants to take you somewhere, and that's not just to heaven when you die, for God can take you there in a moment! The fact remains that God wants to take you somewhere in this life. He has a destiny for your life that involves taking you from where you are right now and bringing you through a process that will sometimes be painful, oftentimes challenging, but will always be fulfilling, and will ultimately lead to the realization of that destiny.

Like Abraham, you might be called to move forward in faith even though you might not know where you are going. You might only know that God is leading the way, but that becomes sufficient for the moment. At other times, you might have more insight that enables you to better understand where God is taking you. But either way there's a Red Sea awaiting you; there's an obstacle standing before you. Yet for those who respond by walking in faith and obedience to the call of God, there is always a way forward to a life of achievement, fulfilment and victory.

However, this will not be fully realized for any of us until we respond positively to the writer to the Hebrew's directive when he said, 'Let us throw off everything that hinders' (Heb 12:1). So whatever it is that is hindering your walk, put it to one side, lay it down and press right in to God's very best for your life. Do so with the same determination of Paul, who said, 'I press on to take hold of that for which Christ Jesus took hold of me' (Phil 3:12).

Legs to run

The apostle Paul said to Timothy, 'I have finished the race' (2 Tim 4:7). He often spoke allegorically of the Christian life as a race, and in the same way he spoke of Christians as athletes. An athlete is a participator as opposed to a spectator, and is someone who wants to be an achiever. It is therefore important for us to acknowledge that God has not called us to a life of faith that simply plants us in a church-building, to be watered and fed once or twice a week. We have not been called to be mere church attendees and mere spectators, but rather we have been called to a life of active discipleship.

We have been called to become students in God's educational system, as Paul said to Timothy, '[Be] a workman who does not need to be ashamed and who correctly handles the word of truth' (2 Tim 2:15), but also to become fully committed followers of Christ, who will pursue Him no matter what the cost; who will stand where He would stand; who will walk where He would walk; who will run as He would run, and will pursue what He would pursue.

The purpose in running is not to make up for lost time or to simply keep pace with others, for we are not in competition against each other, but the purpose is that we might individually and collectively become active participators and achievers within the kingdom of God and that we might become positive contributors to the church and society.

On the one hand the Bible makes it clear that we are in a fight, wrestling against the powers of darkness. It was for this reason that Paul said, 'For our struggle is not against flesh and blood, but against the rulers, against the authorities, against the powers of this dark world and against the spiritual forces of evil in the heavenly realms' (Eph 6:12). But we are also involved in a race for which there is a prize at the end for all who compete and complete. That's why Paul said, 'I press on towards the goal to win the prize for which God has called me heavenwards in Christ Jesus' (Phil 3:14). There is a race to be run and a prize to be won, and by adding legs to our faith we are not only able to stand and not only able to walk, but we are also able to run the race and win the prize.

The prize, however, is not necessarily for taking first place, but for actually finishing the race. For everyone who finishes this race gets the prize. This is why it is so important not only to compete, but also to complete, i.e. to finish. This is achieved by doing it God's way, which is the way of the cross, the way of self-sacrifice. The gun is for losers, but the cross is for winners.

Chapter Five

STEPPING OUT

For ten years I had sensed that God was calling me into full-time Christian service. I knew this meant attending Bible college and then beyond that moving into pastoral ministry. The initial step, in terms of going to Bible college, would prove to be our first Red Sea experience, when Kathleen and I had to step beyond the personal concerns that both of us had at that time about an unknown future.

We were stepping out not knowing where the journey would take us. We knew we were going to the Elim Bible College in Surrey, England, but beyond that we did not know. Two years later, with college training completed, we were making our way back to Northern Ireland. Back to a future and to a ministry that Bible college could not have prepared us for.

We pastored a church for two-and-a-half years in Rathfriland before returning to Belfast in 1982, where we pastored our second church for ten years. However, this was all fairly 'normal' stuff. I was doing all I had been taught to do as far as pastoring a church was concerned, and was doing it all quite well. But in 1989 I once again experienced the call of God that challenged me to move in a new direction. This time it was to do something a little more unusual than simply go off to Bible college. This time it was to purchase an old cinema! This became my second Red Sea experience, but against all the odds I eventually stepped out of my personal comfort zone and crossed that sea in June 1989.

Having raised the funds from several sources, the Stadium cinema was purchased and was converted into the Stadium Youth and Community Centre. It was then we began to reach out to the community in a much greater and much more meaningful way than we had previously done through normal church activities, particularly to young people within the Shankill community. This is explained in much more detail in my first book, *Through Terror and Adversity*, and can be ordered on our website at www.newlifeministriesireland.co.uk or by emailing jack.mckee1@btinternet.com.

However, stepping out does not just mean being willing to attend Bible college, making yourself available to pastor a local church, or even to purchase a cinema, but to be willing to go wherever God would lead and to do whatever He puts within our hearts. Jesus might well have called the paralytic to take up his bed and walk, but there is no such command for the Christian, but rather to leave the bed behind, to leave the comforts of this world and to take up the cross and follow Christ.

Stepping out sometimes means stepping in; sometimes it means stepping into the water or stepping into the fire. When Peter stepped out of the boat, he stepped into the water. When Shadrach, Meshach and Abednego stepped out in obedience to God they stepped into the fire. However, all were to discover that whether it was water or fire, they were not on their own; for Jesus was on the water to take Peter by the hand and to walk him back to the boat, while the three young

Hebrews were joined by a fourth person in the fiery furnace, who is described as one who 'looks like a son of the gods' (Dan 3:25). Just as Peter was able to walk back to the boat, so these three young men were able to walk out of the fire unharmed and without even the smell of smoke on their clothes. God did not promise us a waterless or a fireless life, but on the contrary He said, 'When you pass through the waters, I will be with you; and when you pass through the rivers, they will not sweep over you. When you walk through the fire, you will not be burned' (Is 43:2).

During the following years of ministry God was to call me out of the boat and out of the comfort zone several times. He would call me into situations that were as volatile as walking on water or walking through fire. He would call me to step out of the box and to not only lift the cross in my preaching as a pastor and in my lifestyle as a Christian, but also literally to lift the cross above the gun and to do so in the midst of violence and death.

The Loyalist feud

It was Saturday 19th August 2000. The day had begun quite normally for those living within the Shankill community. There was no sense of imminent danger. Everyone knew that during this particular day there would be a march along the Shankill Road by flute bands and members of the Ulster Freedom Fighters (UFF). But this did not cause anyone to be alarmed, because this was a Protestant community where many of the bandsmen and UFF membership actually lived and socialized. There was no reason to think that anything would go wrong. But go wrong it did, and with such tragic consequences.

As the parade had almost completed its march past the Rex

Bar on the front of the Shankill Road, a serious confrontation erupted between members of the UFF and members of the Ulster Volunteer Force (UVF), who were also from the Shankill community. To this day, both organizations maintain their different interpretations as to what went wrong. However, whatever it was that sparked it off, we nonetheless witnessed the beginning of a new conflict within the Shankill community – a conflict that did not involve Republican terrorists (the IRA, etc.) but one that involved the two most powerful Protestant/Loyalist paramilitary terrorist organizations in Northern Ireland, the UVF and the UFF.

Before the weekend was over, three men had been shot dead. Their families were thrown into sudden and unexpected grief, while seven others had been shot and seriously wounded. Among the dead and injured were those who were known to us personally. Dozens of families had been put out of their homes, while many others fled because they no longer felt safe. A real sense of fear quickly gripped the whole community as the implosion of internal violence rapidly spread across the Shankill from top to bottom and affected virtually every street.

The opposing paramilitaries began to literally tear the community apart. They appeared to be ripping out its heart and throwing it to the wolves. The situation made many of us feel that the Shankill was committing public suicide, but the challenge to all of us was to do something that would help prevent this from happening. So, like others around me, I found myself on the streets visiting church members, friends, family members and some of those who had been directly affected by this sudden outburst of violence.

While I was sitting in the home of friends, speaking with someone who had been directly affected by the violence, I received a phone call from Kathleen. She called to let me know that a young man had been shot dead in the Old Park area of Belfast, an area adjacent to the Shankill community. The young man had apparently been given assurances about his safety, but was tragically shot dead while visiting his girlfriend. Following this and other terrifying events that same evening, I decided it was time for someone from within the community of the church to speak up and speak out for the sake of all the people.

At 1.30 in the morning I made contact with the BBC, who agreed to run a radio interview. I made a public call to church ministers and other church leaders who lived and ministered within our community to meet with me for the purpose of discussing a united response to the downward spiralling situation. Thankfully, at 10 a.m. there was a positive response that led to further television and radio interviews, with a joint statement being read to the media on behalf of the Shankill churches. Within days, many committed Christians joined together for special times of united prayer that no doubt had a positive impact on the whole situation.

Unfortunately, some church leaders did not get involved and did not encourage their people to become involved, while others within the wider community were far from happy that the church was getting involved in this way. Sometimes, and with some people, you just can't win! However, looking at the glass as if it were half full rather than half empty, I was nonetheless delighted that at least there were those within the church community who were trying to do something to help bring the violence to an end.

Yet, for all our efforts, before it was all over there were seven dead, dozens more wounded and hundreds moved from their homes through eviction or through fear. The gun seemed to be prevailing as Protestant turned against Protestant, Loyalist against

Loyalist, neighbour against neighbour, friend against friend; and even family member against family member due to the respective membership of the opposing organizations.

The first Cross Walk

It was during one of our united prayer gatherings that I put out a call for a united peace march along the full length of the Shankill Road. The purpose was to mobilize Christians within the community, including others who would join with them, in a public challenge to the terrorists, calling on them to end the violence that was tearing the community apart. This was to be led upfront by those church ministers and leaders who were supporting this initiative, and was to take place on Saturday 26th August 2000.

However, while all the plans were in place, there were rumours afoot that some of the antagonists were planning to disrupt the march, particularly in the Lower Shankill where our church building is situated. I also began to detect a sense of apprehension among some of our own people. It was at that time I felt the Lord bring a personal challenge to my heart concerning the need to motivate and inspire others, for as Paul said, 'God did not give us a spirit of timidity, but a spirit of power, of love and of self-discipline' (2 Tim 1:7).

I knew it was not enough to simplistically encourage people to exercise their faith and to do so with words only, but they needed to be encouraged with something more tangible. They actually needed to see something that would help motivate and strengthen their faith. The challenge therefore that God brought to me at that time was to pave the way for the united march on Saturday by putting legs on my own faith.

So on Friday morning, the day before the united march, I

chose to walk along the centre of the Shankill Road, from top to bottom, and to do so while carrying a six-foot wooden cross. This was my way of saying, 'Come on! You can do this!' This was something I had never done before. Neither did I know of anyone in Northern Ireland who had ever done such a thing. The only person who came to mind was Arthur Blessitt from the USA, who had walked our streets while carrying a cross way back in 1971/72/73 and finally in 1979. He was my only point of reference, plus the fact that I knew this was something that God had placed in my spirit. I knew what I needed to do; I knew that my faith needed to grow legs and that my faith needed to be actioned.

So, on that particular Friday morning, Kathleen drove me to the Woodvale Park at the top end of the Shankill Road. Finding an appropriate place to stop, she brought the car to a halt, left me off and then quickly drove away, leaving me standing there with a six-foot cross in my hands! It reminded me of a dog that we had once owned called Jip. His previous owner decided she wanted to get rid of him, so she put him in the car and left him off on a remote country lane outside the town of Carrickfergus. Hoping she would never see the dog again, she drove off and left him standing there, totally bewildered, by the side of the road. However, when she finally got back home, there was the dog sitting at her front door waiting for her.

Well, there was I, knowing I would never make it back home before Kathleen even if I had wanted to, standing alone at the top end of the Shankill Road with a six-foot wooden cross, but with a real sense of God's presence and with the amazing feeling that I was not really alone anyway. So, taking a deep breath of the Shankill Road's fresh air, I lifted up that cross and rested the bottom of it on the buckle of my belt. I moved to the centre of the road, and then just began walking down the Shankill between the traffic as it came at me from both directions.

Although this had not been previously publicized, people immediately understood why I was doing this. Many began to respond positively. Motorists sounded their horns in approval. Some rolled down their windows and spoke out to encourage me. This was something I very much appreciated, not to mention needed! Women stood at the edge of the pavement and just looked on as I walked past. The evident sympathetic expressions on many of their faces seemed to say, 'We're with you, Jack.' Some actually called out, 'Well done, Jack.' Others stood and applauded, some with smoke rising from their hands as they held on to the cigarettes that were firmly fixed between their fingers.

Many of these women would have had sons, husbands, fathers and/or brothers who were actively caught up in the feud, with some of them being on opposite sides of the feud due to the organizations to which they belonged. For example, a father might have been in the UVF while his son was in the UFF, or a brother in the UVF and another in the UFF.

As I continued walking along the centre of the road, I noticed several soldiers and two police officers patrolling the area on foot. I thought for sure they would confront me and order me off the road. I began to rehearse in my mind what I might say to them if they approached me, and I wondered if I might even be arrested. As we passed each other by, they being on the pavements on either side of me, my eyes looked nervously into several of theirs, when thankfully one of the police officers smiled at me and gave a nod of approval. This was a reassuring sign that confirmed I was not going to be arrested or even stopped for carrying the cross in such a manner.

The strangest moment, in terms of my personal feelings, was

when I walked past the Rex Bar, where the feud had broken out just days beforehand. It was a warm Friday afternoon and many of the men who would normally have been drinking inside the bar were actually standing outside enjoying the sun, and of course the beer. As I walked past the bar, I saw some of the men take a few steps towards the edge of the pavement. With pint glasses of beer in their hands they stood in silence and looked on as I walked past with the cross. None of them spoke, but all were deep in thought. Some would have been thinking, 'Well done,' while others would have been thinking, 'What an idiot!'

Soon I was crossing the traffic lights that at that time had become the new dividing line that separated the Mid Shankill from the Lower Shankill. As I walked along the Lower Shankill I began to feel a little more apprehensive, but this feeling soon lifted when three women paused on the edge of the footpath to greet me. Each of them applauded, while one quietly said, 'Well done, Jack!' This did not make me feel any sense of self-importance, but it did provide a welcome and timely word of encouragement.

Several minutes later I was finally at the bottom end of the Shankill Road. I had completed my first ever walk while carrying a cross, and did so under very difficult circumstances. It did not matter what others had thought or what they had said about me personally. What mattered was that my faith was not without legs, and that my attempt to encourage and inspire others was not confined to words, or to the inside of a church building, but was public and transparent.

The following day, we were encouraged by the fact that more than 500 people turned up for the march down the Shankill Road. Given the circumstances and the sad decline in the Shankill's population, this was a fair turnout. The march was led by a number of local church ministers and other church leaders, but out in front was one of our own young men, Jamie, who proudly led the way while carrying the same cross that I had carried the day before. The march was well received by others within the community, as many stood along the way and applauded as an expression of their support.

Once again, as we passed the Rex Bar, I noticed some of the men standing silently with pints of beer in their hands. They looked on as we made our way towards the Lower Shankill, but they did so with an apparent look of approval. Soon we had crossed over from the Mid Shankill to the Lower Shankill. Some of us had quietly expected that at this point we might receive some abuse, but thankfully this was not forthcoming. We were later told that some of the 'area commanders' within the Lower Shankill had told their people to stay indoors until the march had passed.

We finally concluded the march at the bottom of the Shankill Road with a brief word of prayer and thanksgiving. We prayed for an end to the ongoing violence that had gripped our community, and prayed for those who had already suffered during those tragic days, particularly for those families who had lost loved ones.

I thank God that many more were bold enough to put legs to their faith that day. Words are great at times, as is preaching, but Isaiah said, 'How beautiful on the mountains are *the feet* of those who bring good news' (Is 52:7, italics mine). We may never know the full extent of all that was accomplished that day. However, we do know that the 'ordinary' people had been given an opportunity to speak out and that many did so; we know the churches had been given an opportunity to come together in a worthwhile common cause and that several did so; we know that the march did not go unnoticed, but that it made an impact at that moment and on that day; and we know that the cross had been lifted above the gun in the midst of a bloody feud and as a public challenge to those behind the violence to desist. We know we did something!

The ending of the feud

I firmly believe that because of the lead given by those churches that had rallied together during those days of prayer and witness, along with the efforts of others within our community and including those of influence within the feuding organizations, the violence finally subsided. I pay tribute to all who made a positive contribution in helping to find a way forward at that time. Sadly, however, the feud had managed to spread to north Belfast, where others were to die before it eventually came to an end.

While not wanting to add to the negative perceptions that many have of the Shankill, I have to say that although the feuding has ended, the community has never properly recovered from the insanity of those days. During the following weeks and months many continued to leave the Shankill in search of the elusive peace and of better trade, employment and education opportunities. However, many remain in the hope that things will improve in the long term. As a ministry within the Shankill community, we did what we could at that time, and we continue to work for the good of all.

For myself, I never thought I would ever lift the cross again in such a manner, but God was later to confront me with an even greater challenge: to once again carry the cross, although not for one day only, but for 40 days. This challenge would also include carrying the cross through both the Protestant Shankill and the neighbouring Catholic Falls communities; two communities that have been divided by a 20-foot high concrete wall and have been warring against each other for more than 30 years.

I have faced many challenges over the years and believe I have responded well to most of them, but this I think was the greatest and most frightening of them all. This was my greatest personal Red Sea experience ever, but I knew that for every Red Sea there is a way made by God that is so miraculous we don't even get our feet wet when we step out in obedience. Don Moen's song 'God will make a way' always reminds me of this. Don reminds us that God makes a way when it seems impossible, working in ways we don't see. In the midst of it all God is our guide, showing us His love and giving us strength.

Chapter Six

LIFTING THE CROSS ABOVE THE GUN

Often when I am away ministering elsewhere, particularly in the USA, I will take time to reflect and to pray about our work back home. It was during a visit to Colorado in October 2001 that the Lord began to challenge me about doing a 40-day Cross Walk in Belfast. Such thoughts first began when Steve Carroll, an intercessor at the New Life Church, Colorado Springs, shared with me the need to lift up the cross in my preaching. I did not take this as a criticism, but as a challenge to focus more on the cross during that time of my ministry. The more I thought and prayed about this, the more God challenged me not only to do what Steve had said, but to actually and literally lift up the cross within the streets of Belfast, and to do so for 40 days.

The aim of the walk

The aim of the walk would be to lift up the cross in such a way that it would focus the attention of the people on the greatest historical and religious symbol in world history. The concrete wall that literally stands between our communities is a symbol of division and hatred, but the cross is a symbol of reconciliation and love. However, the Cross Walk would not be about promoting the need to reconcile religions, but rather it would highlight the need for people to be reconciled to God through the cross. For only then, when people are truly reconciled to God, does it become possible for reconciliation proper to take place between those who are divided.

Where and how

So, having prayed hard and long, I finally accepted the challenge. Essentially I decided to walk from our New Life Fellowship church at the bottom of the Shankill Road, through a gate in the dividing wall and into the neighbouring Catholic community. Here I would walk along the centre of the Falls Road, onto the Springfield Road, through another gate in the dividing wall in Lanark Way and back down the Protestant Shankill Road, finishing back at the New Life Church. I would walk along the centre section of each road, holding the cross high on my chest, using a carpenter's belt to hold it in place.

Many others offered to walk with me. Some of those offers came from as far away as Alabama and California, USA. However, I believed this was God's challenge to me personally and that if others joined with me they effectively would turn what was meant to be a lone Cross Walk into a procession. This would have raised further issues here in Northern Ireland and would have reduced the impact of a lone walk with the cross as its focus.

Concerns

I did not have any serious concerns about my own personal security and safety, although others might have had such concerns on my behalf. It was possible that there might well have been some within the Catholic community who would have taken offence at a 'Protestant' minister walking along their streets, cross or no cross. This was certainly something I had seriously considered and had prepared myself for.

By the same token, there might well have been those within the Protestant community who could have taken offence at being reminded of their need to be reconciled to God and to others. The challenge to both communities was to look to the cross rather than the gun. However, I simply did not know what kind of reception I would receive in either community. I was therefore ready for anything!

Confirmation

God had prepared me for this over and over again by confirming clearly that this was His direct challenge to me at that time and that He had not only gone before me, but would be walking alongside me every step of the way. For example, I had planned not to publicize the fact that I was going to be doing the 40-Day Cross Walk until Sunday 10th February 2002, which was only eight days prior to the first day of the walk. However, the very day before my big announcement in church, something happened that caused me concern. This resulted in me telling Kathleen that I would not be going ahead with the walk. It seemed it was over before it had even begun.

Ten minutes later I was checking my email when I received a

message from a brother who runs a radio station in the USA. He concluded his message with the words, 'I am praying for you, that you will continue to carry the banner of the cross in Northern Ireland.' This brother knew nothing of what I had been planning, never mind what I was experiencing at that very moment. I looked at this and thought, 'Wow!' I could hardly believe what I was reading. If ever I needed a final piece of confirmation, this surely was it. Within moments I was back with Kathleen telling her that the Cross Walk was back on again.

Reconciliation

There are those who believe they can achieve peace through the barrel of a gun, but I thank God for the more positive efforts that are taking place across Northern Ireland to promote peace and reconciliation between our divided people. These efforts, whether they come through the church or through other legitimate groups within the community, help our people, from whatever religious or political persuasion, to at least believe in the possibility of peace.

However, it is my belief that the cross is more powerful than the gun, and even more powerful than community programmes and projects, and that people of all colours, cultures and religious persuasions can only properly be reconciled to each other by first being reconciled to God through the cross.

This does not disparage those efforts to reconcile at a human level, but God has called us first to be reconciled to Him, knowing that a positive consequence of this will be the breaking down of all other dividing walls. As Paul said, 'For he [Christ] himself is our peace, who has . . . destroyed the barrier, the dividing wall of hostility' (Eph 2:14). If He can break down the dividing wall that stands between Him and us, then surely He can remove the wall that stands between fellow humans.

The wall is coming down

As the Berlin Wall came down in 1991, it is my desire, like that of most other people living in Northern Ireland, that the Belfast Wall would likewise come down. I believe and hope that I will see this in my own lifetime. However, the wall is serving a purpose, in keeping opposing communities apart and protecting them from each other. The Berlin Wall divided families and friends, whereas the Belfast Wall keeps enemies apart.

When the Berlin Wall finally came down, people from both sides of the wall ran to each other. They hugged and kissed each other. They laughed, they wept and they danced with joy that such a monstrosity was finally breached and that estranged families and friends could now be reunited. I can tell you that if the Belfast Wall were to come down people would not be running across to embrace, hug and kiss each other.

I pray hard and long for the day when the dividing wall in Belfast will come down, and I want to be there when it does. But I pray even more for the pulling down of every wall of division and hatred that exists in the hearts and minds of many within Northern Ireland; for these are the real dividing walls; those that exists in our minds and in our hearts.

Pre-prayer walk

A few days prior to the commencement of the 40-Day Cross Walk I decided to do a lone prayer walk following the same route I would soon take with the cross. With some apprehension, I began to walk along the Falls Road. I had never walked this way before and did not know what to expect. I wondered whether anyone would recognize me. And if so, how would they react?

While these thoughts were going through my mind, I began to walk past a British Telecom truck that was sitting in front of me on the actual pavement. While I was passing the truck I heard someone call out to me with the question, 'Are you lost?' he shouted. My immediate thought was that someone had indeed recognized me as being from 'the other side'. With a slight hesitation I looked around to respond, and there sitting in the cab of the truck was Billy Potts, one of our prayer intercessors in New Life Fellowship! This was not just a relief to me; it was such an encouragement. I believed that by his very presence at that specific moment in time, Billy was a messenger sent from God to let me know that I was not doing this walk on my own, but that the ministering angels of God would be watching over me every step of the way.

As I continued to walk along the Falls Road I quietly prayed for the coming Cross Walk. I also inwardly sang a few worship songs, which helped me to focus more on God and less on the fact that I was walking along the Falls Road, and on my own at that. I did get to speak to a few people along the way, even if it was only to say, 'Hello.' I am not sure if anyone really did recognize me, but it was difficult to ignore those who looked at me with the kind of look that seemed to say, 'I think I know you from somewhere!'

Before long I was passing through the gates in Lanark Way and was finally onto the top end of the Shankill Road. As I walked back towards the church I could clearly feel the presence of God. I knew that God was with me and would be with me in the coming weeks. For the first time the sense of excitement was beginning to rise. I had completed the lone prayer walk along the Falls Road and the Shankill Road. The next time I would walk this way, it would be in the centre of the road and with a seven-foot cross.

A copy of the route map was emailed to many who joined with me in prayer during the 40 days of the Cross Walk. Prayer partners were asked to pray for the walk as a whole, but also to take time to pray specifically for each street, and each house along the route, and for each resident who lived within both communities. They were also invited to pray for the anointing of the Holy Spirit upon each step that would be taken along the way.

- The starting and finishing point was New Life Fellowship Church at the corner of Townsend Street and Peter's Hill at the bottom end of the Shankill Road.
- From here it was through the first gate in the 'Peace Wall' and into the Catholic community. Then it was up along Divis Street and along the Falls Road.
- From here I would turn into the Springfield Road, where I would walk to Lanark Way, at which point I would walk through another gate in the 'Peace Wall' and back into the Protestant community.
- Finally it would be back to the Shankill Road, where I would make my way downhill and back to New Life Fellowship at the bottom, from whence my journey had begun.

During the preparation period there was one thing I had almost forgotten, and was therefore left until the last minute, and that was police approval. I had talked to God about it. I had talked to Kathleen about it. I had talked to friends about it. I had talked to the church about it. But I had not talked to the police about it! In fact, I only made contact with the local police station four days before the commencement of the walk.

The police officer took note of my 'strange request' and said he would respond before the end of the day. What he did not tell me was that my request had to be put before the Northern Ireland Parades Commission. However, there was a problem: the members of the Parades Commission were all in South Africa at that time.

Unknown to me the police actually made contact with the Parades Commission in South Africa. They were able to look at my request and to make a decision that permitted me to walk as planned. I was told that the decision was made on the basis that 'one man does not constitute a march'. It was therefore put back to the police for them to make a decision on the basis of personal and road-safety issues. The police were willing to approve the Cross Walk, provided I used wisdom and watched out for myself and for the motorists, who could very well panic seeing some guy walking along the centre of the road carrying a cross.

Another problem was that some of the gates in the wall between the communities were closed at nights and weekends. This would present me with a difficulty on both Saturday and Sunday morning. So I talked with the police again, who were happy to resolve the problem by providing me with a key to open one of the gates and guaranteed that the other gate would be opened when I needed to pass through to the Shankill on my return. Talk about the Gates of Hell not prevailing! It was as if God was making sure that all of the hindrances were removed and that the route would be accessible. Everything was now in place and I was all but ready to commence the walk.

Chapter Seven

LIFTING THE CROSS
ABOVE THE WALL

It was Monday 18th February 2002. This was the day I had decided to commence the Cross Walk. For the next 40 days I would be following a route that would take me through our divided communities and around the physical wall that stands as a concrete symbol of that division. Two of my main concerns were that the cross would get heavier with every step I took, and also that I might have given myself a much bigger physical challenge than I had first thought. However, by the commencement of the walk I had let many friends and prayer partners across the world know what I would be doing, so by the first day of the walk, prayers and messages of support were arriving from various parts of the world via email. These all served to strengthen me. So much so that when I had finally completed my first day's walk, I felt I could go on and do it all over again!

Having left from New Life Fellowship Church, within minutes I was walking through the first security gate of the dividing wall and onto Divis Street, which led to the Falls Road on the other side of the wall. As this was my first day of the walk, I was immediately conscious of people's bewilderment at the sight of someone walking along the centre of the road carrying a cross with 'JOHN 3:16' written across it. This was typified by one young Catholic lad, about eleven or twelve years of age, who took a step towards the edge of the pavement and very seriously called out, 'Hey, John! What are you doing?'

His question brought a welcome smile to my face, but also a touch of sadness to my heart as I considered the implications of his question, not only for him, but also for the entire community through which I was walking. I briefly explained to him that my name was Jack and that John is a book in the Bible, with a verse that tells us how much God loves us and that Jesus died for us. He looked quite bemused, and made me wonder how many more would be just like him. How many more would not know anything about the most famous and the best known verse in the entire Bible? But what an opportunity to share it!

Anyway, I proceeded along the planned route, which took me through part of the Catholic community on the Falls Road and then back through another security gate in the dividing wall that would take me back to the Protestant Shankill Road, and finally back to New Life at high noon.

My biggest problem during this first day of the walk was not the people, but having to contend with the physical elements. I had to fight against the wind in order to hold the cross steady and upright, but the people on both sides of the wall were magnanimous with their courteousness, particularly the motorists. Even though at this stage the people had no idea why I was doing this, nor for how long, yet they waved from their cars and sounded their horns in welcome approval, while others rolled down their car windows and spoke words of encouragement, making me feel somewhat at ease.

However, there was still a long way to go. This was only Day 1 of 40 days; there were still 39 to go! I reminded myself of the words of Jesus when He said, 'Do not worry about tomorrow' (Mt 6:34). I knew the first day was a good day and that I should not worry about all the tomorrows that seemed to be awaiting me, so I began to move forward with a sense of excitement and expectancy. I did not know what the next 39 days would bring forth, but I did know that what I was doing at that time, I was truly doing for God and for Ulster.

Jesus died for gypsies

The following day, Tuesday 19th February, I once again set off as I had done the day before, only this time I was wondering how the people would react when they saw me back again! No sooner had I crossed through the first gate and back onto the Falls Road, when I was approached by a couple of Irish gypsies, who called out to me from their van and said, 'Hey, what's that you're doing?' I immediately stopped and took a moment to explain not only what I was doing, for it was quite obvious that I was carrying a cross, but also why I was doing such a thing.

I briefly shared John 3:16 with these two men while they sat in their van with the window rolled down. It was quite obvious that this was the first time these two men had heard about John 3:16 and that they did not know where it was or what it was. I finished by saying to them, 'I'm just wanting people to know that God still loves them!' With a distinct Irish/Romany brogue they wished me 'the luck o' the Irish' and drove off to the sound of me calling out, 'God Bless you men.'

Now just in case someone might be reading this book and wondering, 'Well, where in fact is this John 3:16 and what is it?' let me explain that John is the fourth book in the New Testament of the Bible. The sixteenth verse of the third chapter is perhaps the best known verse in the entire Bible and is written as follows: 'For God so loved the world that he gave his one and only Son, that whoever believes in him shall not perish but have eternal life.' When John speaks of God, he is speaking of the God of the Bible, the Maker of heaven and earth. When he speaks of 'his one and only Son', he is speaking of Jesus Christ, who came from heaven to earth and was crucified for the sins of the world, so that whoever (that's you and me) believes in Him (that is Jesus) will not perish, but will have eternal life. Quite simply put, God loved us and Jesus died for us.

Having left the gypsies, I continued to make my way along the Falls Road when two young Catholic men pulled up in a car alongside me and, like the gypsies, asked me what I was doing. Once again I had the joy of sharing John 3:16 and explained to these young men the need for a divided people not only to be reconciled to each other, but also to be personally reconciled to God. (Most people in Northern Ireland understand the meaning of reconciliation.)

Things were going well, until a few moments later, when a very irate driver of a black taxi yelled from his cab window, 'Away onto the Shankill with that, ya ****!' Little did he know I had only just come from the Shankill and was in fact making my way back to the Shankill via the Falls and Springfield Roads! I knew this was 'his road' and that I was only a visitor walking through. I also knew this was only my second day of the walk, and that not everyone was yet aware of the fact that this crazy guy from the Shankill was walking through both communities and would be doing so for 40 days.

As I made my way past the Springfield Road police station I was looking ahead when I noticed a group of men standing on both sides of the road. The closer I got to them, the more concerned I became. As I began to pass them some of them began to shout angrily at me, 'Away back to the Shankill, ya header!' (A header in this context in Northern Ireland means 'an idiot'.) They obviously knew I was from the Shankill, but I had already determined that I would not respond or react to any negative comments. So I never looked right or left. I just kept on walking straight ahead along the centre of the road without wavering.

When I walked through the gates at Lanark Way, I noticed a car that had followed me from the Catholic side of the wall. It drove alongside me for a short distance. There was a man in the driver's seat and a woman sitting next to him. The driver rolled down his window and said, 'Fair play to ya, mate.' He then turned his car around and drove back towards the Falls Road. My instinct was that he had followed me to see if I really was going to walk the Protestant side as well, and on seeing that I was he made his comment and then drove back the way he had come, giving me one final wave.

Five minutes later I was on my way back down the Shankill Road. The local cobbler, who had stood at the front door of his shop on the first day and had quietly watched me walk by with the cross, was there again on this second day of the walk. This time he called out to me, 'Hey Jack, I'll do your soles and heels for you when you need them done!' I smiled and said, 'You never know, I might just take you up on that,' although I never did, as I was wearing trainers! A little further on I heard one woman say to another, 'At least he's got guts!' Soon, after several hand waves and welcome comments, I was back at the church and ready for a well-deserved bowl of home-made vegetable soup.

God in the shadows

Early the next morning I checked the weather forecast. It was frightening! It spoke of heavy rain and gale force winds between 50 and 70 m.p.h. – not a good day for cross-walkers, or headers! To make matters worse, before I actually left home to make my way to the church the bad weather had already begun to kick in, complete with visuals and sound effects – flashes of lightning followed by bursts of thunder. Later, when I stepped outside the church and onto the road with the cross, it was still raining, so I put my hood up and began to walk directly into the rain and towards the Falls Road.

Amazingly, before I got to the end of the street, the rain had suddenly stopped and the sun was beginning to break through the clouds. Later, as I approached the Shankill Road from Lanark Way, the sky began to darken again. Yet as I walked onto the Shankill Road, the dark clouds just seemed to move away and the sun continued to shine. As I walked through the threatening storm, I was doing my best to encourage myself. I was even singing to myself the greatest football song that is connected to the greatest football team in world history (Liverpool FC), 'You'll never walk alone'.

Of course I had also been talking to God and praying that it would not rain and that the wind would not get too strong. Like Elijah, I had looked for God in the midst of these things, but it was hard for me to see or to hear Him. However, as I began to make my way down the Shankill Road I was amazed to see the shadow of the cross stretching out in front of me on the road. It reminded me of an old song we used to sing in church, 'Standing somewhere in the shadows you'll find Jesus'. It also reassured me of God's presence and of the knowledge that He was indeed with me, and that He would be going before me and before every step of this Cross Walk.

Anyway, as I walked through the streets that day, and in spite of the weather conditions, it seemed that a newspaper report on the Cross Walk had helped the atmosphere. The *Belfast Telegraph*, our main daily newspaper, had carried a story of the Cross Walk and a photograph. Later, the *Andersontown News*, read by many Catholics within the Falls community, would also carry a helpful story on the Cross Walk. They not only had a photograph of me walking along the road with the cross, but they also referred to me as 'the Holy Man from the Shankill'. I did not know that we had such people living on the Shankill Road, least of all that I should be considered one of them! Of course I jest, for I do know the root meaning of the word 'holy'. However, I have to truly admit that I was a little surprised that a Catholic newspaper should refer to anyone from the Shankill as 'holy'.

There is no doubt in my mind that these reports helped to reduce the amount of barracking within the Falls community, and to create a greater sense of awareness in both communities of the fact that I would not just be walking for a few days, but for 40 days. If the people did not know it before, they would certainly know it now.

As I walked along the Springfield Road a car pulled up alongside me. The man who was driving asked the question, 'Is everything OK? Are things quiet enough for you?' I replied, 'Yes, great thanks!' He wished me well and immediately drove on ahead of me. He turned into Lanark Way and into the Protestant community. Soon after this I was starting my walk along Lanark Way and was making my way towards the Shankill Road when this same car came back through the security gates. The driver gave me a wave and drove back towards the Falls Road and into the Catholic community. I immediately thought this very strange, and wondered what was behind it. I was left with nothing but my thoughts, although I was to meet him again sometime later.

However, things were to lighten up a little when I got back to the Shankill Road. Besides the now routine hand gestures and verbal greetings, I remember passing a number of people who were standing at a bus stop. I could hear one elderly lady clearly say to those standing next to her, 'Why doesn't he go and get himself a job?' I must admit that this even brought a smile to my face.

However, notwithstanding the above challenges, this was another good day and another good walk of witness. People's thoughts were once again focused, even if momentarily, upon the cross with the inscription JOHN 3:16, and not so much on the messenger who simply carried the cross. This was my prayer and my objective – that people would see less of me and more of the cross.

Fair-weather Christians

Before leaving for the walk each day, I would have a couple of people pray with me. These would normally be Jim McAuley, a good stalwart within New Life Fellowship, and Robert Spiers, who is married to Kathleen's sister Sally, and also a great personality within the church. Robert was at one time a member of the UDA, but he was saved in New Life Fellowship back in 2000. During his time in the UDA Robert would often talk about 'fair-weather Loyalists'! So when he was praying for me at the beginning of the fourth day, he prayed, 'Lord, if it rains it rains. Just let the people see that we're not fair-weather Christians!' Well, I can tell you that the Lord answered Robert's prayer – I got soaked! But what an honour nonetheless!

To be fair, the weather was not that bad, for it only rained when I was walking down the Shankill Road, but man did it rain! However, the reception in both communities was again markedly improved. There was absolutely no barracking from anyone. There was no one shouting at me to go back to the Shankill Road, and no one calling me an idiot of one description or another! Instead, there were more hand waves, more horns blowing and more encouraging comments such as 'God bless you, son!' But best of all, no one suggested I should go and do a day's work!

One of the things worth mentioning is that while walking down the Shankill Road towards the church I could hear someone call out, 'Hey Jack!' I looked around and there was a man sitting in the driver's side of a car, with another man stepping out of the passenger side. The driver called out to me and said, 'We've been driving around looking for you. We want to take a couple of photographs.' I shouted back across the road at him, 'Where are you from?' He spoke back as quietly as he could, but loud enough for me to hear, 'The *Andersonstown News*.'

On hearing this I immediately responded with, 'Shush! You don't want to say that too loud around here!' When they had quickly taken some photographs, one of them said, 'You're doing a great job, Jack. Keep it up,' and then off they went. Moments later I was back at the church, satisfied that this had been another positive day of witness.

What does John 3:16 mean?

Friday 22nd February and Day 5 of the Cross Walk, but things today would be somewhat different, certainly from the previous two days. I will not focus so much on the negatives, but on the positives, of which there were many. Walking along the centre of the Falls Road I was once again warmly greeted by motorists and pedestrians alike. A white van stopped and the driver simply said, 'Fair play to you, Jack. The Falls is proud of you.' I thanked him and wished him well. I was beginning to realize that I was slowly but surely being accepted on the Falls Road in spite of the fact that I was a Protestant minister from the Shankill Road.

Soon after this another driver called out, 'Fair play to you, mate.' Then from another car that had come from behind, I heard a voice call out, 'God bless you, pastor. It's great to be saved!' To me he was a stranger, but there was obviously something that united both of us.

While all this was going on I had to pause several times because of the strong winds, but soon I was on the Springfield Road, fighting the winds and heading towards Lanark Way. With this being a Friday, there was much more traffic on the road. This made things more difficult, particularly on the Springfield Road, which is quite narrow. Numerous times I had to turn sideways and pretend I was thin, or just walk off to the pavement until one or two high-sided trucks got past. But soon I was walking along Lanark Way and heading again towards the Shankill.

However, just as I was turning into Lanark Way, I was approached by one of the workmen who had stood watching me since Monday from a building site on the Springfield Road. He walked right into the centre of the road to meet with me as I approached the turning point. I did not know what to expect. I actually thought he might be coming to tell me not to come back this way. But my concern was unfounded, for when he spoke to me he said, 'We've been watching you all week, and we want to know if you'd tell us why you're doing this and what JOHN 3:16 means.'

Wow! For me this was what it was all about. First of all I was once again saddened to discover that here were men who did not know anything about JOHN 3:16, but then I was delighted to be able to explain it to him as we stood in the centre of the road while his friends looked on from the building site. As I walked away from him I prayed that as he conveyed my words to his workmates the Spirit of God would reveal the truth of God's love to their hearts. I then thought to myself that if for no other reason, this conversation made the Cross Walk worthwhile.

When I finally crossed through the dividing wall and into Lanark Way, I was once again asked the same question, but this time by five young Protestant men. I walked onto the pavement and stood alongside them and talked with them for a while. As I approached them I asked, 'Do none of you know what JOHN 3:16 means?' One of the young men spoke up and said, 'Yeah, I do.' He then made a good attempt at reciting the entire verse to his friends.

I then took the opportunity to explain exactly what the verse meant about God's love for them as well as for Catholics on the other side of the wall. They seemed to accept this much easier than the fact that I had in reality walked along the Falls Road carrying a cross. Both of these encounters, with the Protestant young men and the Catholic workmen, made me feel so glad I had put 'JOHN 3:16' on the cross.

Well, I don't quite know why, but once again when I got to the Shankill Road the heavens opened. I mean it rained, it snowed, it hailed and it stormed. It was so bad that I had to lift the cross down and place it over my shoulder. I tried to continue walking with the cross, only this time trailing it over my shoulder, but after it had been caught several times by the wind and almost pulled me in front of oncoming traffic, I decided to stop off at the side of the road and wait for the weather to abate.

As I stood behind the cross, shielding myself from the hail and snow, but now completely drenched, a man called out to me from Alpha Taxis. He invited me in for a mug of hot tea until I dried off and the weather changed. I gladly accepted the invitation and within moments I was leaning the cross against a wall inside Alpha Taxis and was drinking a good Shankill Road mug of hot tea while chatting with the owner and some of the workers. This was a welcome and quite friendly break, and certainly was much appreciated on my part.

I believe that God helped me use this situation to nurture a relationship, and at the time I remember thinking to myself that this was well worth the rain and the hail! Ten minutes later, and a 'good' ten minutes in many respects, the weather had turned for the better and I was soon walking down a sunny Shankill Road. Physically, this was my hardest day so far, but it was worth every step and every hailstone, for although not directly connected to this, within less than twelve months one of the taxi drivers and one of the receptionists from this very depot became committed Christians through the ministry of New Life Fellowship. They now attend the church.

Where there is no way

Looking out from my bedroom window on the morning of Saturday 23rd February I was horrified to see an inch of snow covering our street. I listened again to the weather forecast, which is something I did daily during those days. The forecast predicted more snow accompanied by gale force winds. It was not looking good. However, by the time I set out for the walk the sky had cleared to a bright blue and the sun was again sitting proudly in its designated place in the sky, which is just above the Shankill Road.

This being a Saturday meant that the first security gate I normally went through would be closed. This particular gate closes on Friday afternoon each week and is not opened again until Monday morning. However, the police had given me permission to walk along this route for 40 days, knowing it would take me through this and one other security gate. So to make sure I got through this first gate on Saturdays and Sundays, the police actually gave me a key!

My brother-in-law Robert, whom I mentioned earlier, had volunteered to drive around to the other side of the gate where the lock was located. He would open the gate on Saturdays and Sundays so I could walk through and continue with the walk. This confirmed to me that in every and in any situation God will miraculously make a way where there seems to be no way, but that sometimes He will simply get us a key! Peter might well have got the keys of Heaven and Hell, but I had got the key to the gates between the Shankill and the Falls!

As I walked along the Falls Road I was not only greeted by some of the locals with hand waves and horns sounding, but there was an additional welcoming face. It was Denis from our church. He was standing on the pavement waiting for me, as he had previously done on Day 3. I appreciated him being there, and also his company as he walked parallel to me on the pave- ment. Denis had made a personal commitment to follow Christ during his second visit to New Life Fellowship. Other members of his family had done likewise, including his wife Mary, his mother Maggie, who is now in heaven, his sister and his son, whose wife had already committed her life to Christ.

As I walked alone along the centre of the road, Denis would

follow alongside me, but on the pavement. This presented him with several opportunities to share with bewildered passers-by. They would often ask the same question, 'What does John 3:16 mean?' One elderly man on the Falls Road was the first to ask this question of Denis, followed by a young man and his mother at the corner of the Falls and Springfield Roads.

So this was not just about me carrying a cross. It was also about people like Robert, who was willing to cross the divide to ensure that the gate was open for me to walk through, and people like Denis, who was willing to walk on 'the other side' of the wall and to be a witness for Christ. At one time, both of these men would have been willing to lift up a gun. Robert had been a member of the UDA, while Denis was a 'real' soldier in the Irish Rifles, a regiment in the British Army. Yet here they were, doing what they could in order to ensure that the cross was lifted above sectarianism, above the dividing wall and above the gun. However, I know full well that both Robert and Denis would affirm with me that it was not about us, but about lifting up the One who willingly died for all of us, whether Protestant or Catholic, Jew or Muslim, black or white.

However, things were surprisingly much quieter on this day than I had anticipated. There was not as much traffic on the road, which made walking much easier. Neither were there as many people around as I thought there might have been given that this was a popular shopping day. Yet there were still enough people around with whom I could share the message of John 3:16.

Cheers of affirmation

For some reason I had assumed that Sunday would be somewhat uneventful. I assumed that people would either be in church while I was doing the walk, or that many more would be just taking their ease at home or even in bed. There was certainly less traffic on the roads, making it easier for me to more freely exchange greetings with people on the footpaths. These exchanges were very positive.

Although the pubs are officially closed on Sundays in Northern Ireland – not that I would know much about pubs – I was nonetheless amazed to see men knocking on the front or the side doors of some pubs as I walked along the Falls Road. They would glance at me, with some looking bewildered and others looking affirmative. Soon the locked doors were opened and in they would go, with the doors being quickly closed behind them.

As I passed one of these pubs, several men, about five or six of them, came out. I heard them shouting, and knew they were shouting at me. From the corner of my eye I could see one of them running towards me. I looked around, expecting to get a pint of Guinness on the side of the head, and there standing next to me was a young man in his mid-twenties. He had stopped on the edge of the pavement right beside me. As I looked at him I was still unsure what I should expect and wondered what he was up to. I was therefore surprised when he said, 'Well done, mate. Keep it up!' I can tell you, this not only encouraged me, but it caused me to breathe a welcome sigh of relief!

Soon I was going through the gate and onto the Shankill Road. I was back at New Life Fellowship in time for our morning service that started then at 12 noon, although we now meet at 11.00 a.m. and 6.45 p.m. every Sunday.

Chapter Eight

SHOE LEATHER AND SWEAT

After a relatively easy weekend, it was back to the busy roads at the beginning of the second week. Once again I was well received by many on both sides of the wall, although it was obvious that some people still did not know my name because they would shout at me and call me some kind of header! Again let me explain what a header is, especially within the context of cross-walking within Northern Ireland.

A header is someone who is perceived by others to be somewhat strange: someone who is two sandwiches short of a picnic. To be called a header means someone thinks you're an idiot. So in a Belfast context based on the comments of some, a header is not someone who totes a gun, but someone who carries a cross! I wonder what the 'Irish' of the fifth century thought of Patrick! But to look at the biblical perspective, David said, 'The fool [header] says in his heart, "There is no God"' (Psalm 14:1).

However, as I continued with the walk, I was once again amazed that I had to respond to hand waves from taxi drivers on the Falls Road and likewise from taxi drivers on the Shankill Road, the significance of which only people in Belfast would really understand. For taxi drivers on both sides of the dividing wall have always been perceived to be members of, or at least supportive of, paramilitary organizations within their respective communities. Yet here they were, unknown to each other, waving with approval at the same thing: they were waving at a man carrying a cross!

A lorry driver pulled up alongside me on the Falls Road and spoke to me from his cab. He asked, 'How many pairs of shoes have you worn out?' He then went on to ask me how many days I had left and where I would actually be walking. This again showed that people across both communities were very much intrigued by what I was doing. People were obviously talking, and most of it seemed to be positive.

Not just for me

One thing I was always thankful for was the constant flow of encouragement, particularly through email. Every time I went to the computer it seemed to shout out at me, 'Keep on going, Jack. We're praying for you; we're with you!' Messages were coming in from across Ireland, North and South; from across Scotland, Wales, England and other parts of Europe; from Africa, Australia, New Zealand and many of the states across the USA. I was particularly encouraged to receive messages of support from Arthur Blessitt, who is known worldwide for carrying the cross.

In one of these emails someone asked, 'How big is your vision, Jack?' Someone else said, 'Jack, you do not know how big this thing will become!' Another said, 'Jack, not only are you walking there in your homeland, you are actually walking through the streets and communities of every town your daily report reaches.'

On what was now the ninth day, I was once again fighting against the wind and struggling to ensure that the cross was held high. I would purposefully remind myself of the messages of support and of the prayers of so many people from around the world. I reminded myself that I was not now on my own and that I was not doing this just for me, in terms of my obedience to God, but I was doing this for so many others. I was doing this for those who walked with me in spirit through their prayers and messages of support. It seemed they were depending on me to complete the Cross Walk. This was not just my walk any more, but this was their walk. Such thoughts would help to motivate and strengthen me, and would keep me looking beyond where I was at any given moment to the finishing post – no matter how many days ahead it still lay.

Pope John Paul and Pastor Jack!

As I walked along the Falls Road a woman stepped out in front of me. With a camera in her hand she said, 'Would you mind stopping for a moment so I can take your picture?' While I knew that my mission was to lift up the cross and to lift up Christ, I nonetheless paused for a moment and allowed her to take my photograph. I then thought to myself, 'Maybe my photo will end up in her living room alongside the Pope!' I began to imagine what it might look like to have Pope John Paul and Pastor Jack hanging there together in someone's home. I further imagined someone walking into the home and asking the question, 'Who's that beside Pastor Jack?' I then thought to myself, 'Well, at least when she looks at her wall she will not only see John Paul II, but more to the point she will also see JOHN 3:16!'

A little further along the Falls Road a Catholic nun came out from behind the gates of a religious building. She came right into the centre of the road to greet me. With a huge smile on her face she shook my hand and said, 'Thanks for doing what you are doing. We all think it's great, and may God bless you for this.' She then invited me into the building for some tea, but I graciously declined, because I could not afford to drink too much fluid while walking. Having wished each other well, I continued with the walk.

Again, just a little further along the Falls Road, a Catholic man in his fifties called out to me at the top of his voice, 'Well done, Pastor; Keep it going, my friend!' I shouted back my appreciation as I turned into the Springfield Road. Soon I was walking along Lanark Way and heading back towards the Shankill.

At this point three young men approached me. One of them said, 'Hey mister, what are you doing?' After I had explained to them exactly what I was doing, one of them asked, 'Do you really believe in God then?' My response was, 'Yes, I believe in God. That's why I'm carrying this cross, because I want others to think of God also, if only for a moment.' He then asked, 'Do you think it will work?' I answered by saying, 'Well, you're thinking of Him right now, aren't you!' He stood speechless at that point, but smiled at me.

I wished them well and continued with the walk, knowing that once again people were being challenged not only to look to a seven-foot wooden cross, but to look higher to a God who gave His Son as an expression of His love for them.

If only for one

Day 10 was my first major milestone, for not only had I reached double figures, but I had completed one quarter of this glorious challenge. However, fighting against strong winds was still my main concern. It is one thing to attempt walking the white line on the centre of the road while trying to avoid being hit by traffic coming at you from both sides, but it's another thing entirely to walk along the middle of the road while carrying a seven-foot cross in strong winds! My daily prayer was for the wisdom of Solomon and the strength of Samson. I felt I needed both!

While pushing the cross against the wind, I was again delighted to see Denis standing waiting for me as I walked along the Falls Road. Just the sight of him helped to spur me on. Again there were the usual greetings. One that continues to stand out is that of a young Catholic man who stopped his car beside me. The first thing he said to me was, 'Hey mister, are you a header?' (Note what I said above about 'header'). I responded, 'No, I'm Jack McKee.' He then said again, 'Are you not a header?' I responded laughingly, 'No, I'm Jack McKee, and I'm here to tell you that God loves you and that Jesus died for you.' Then with a very serious look on his face he said, 'The only one who ever died for me was my ma, when she opened her legs and gave me birth!' I felt my heart go out to him and I said, 'I'm sorry to hear that, but you need to know that God loves you.' I pointed to JOHN 3:16 printed on the cross and told him what it meant. I was still standing in the middle of the road while he sat in his car next to me, but the traffic was building up behind him and he needed to get going. I wished him well and said to him, 'God bless you, mate.' He replied as he drove off, 'And God bless you too!'

I then made my way along the Springfield Road, waving to people and shaking hands that came out to meet me from cars and vans. Soon I was doing much the same along the Shankill Road and back to New Life, knowing that many had again been touched by the message of the cross, but with the thought that if this was only for the young man in the car, it was worth every step.

I kept on walking

The following day there was much the same kind of reception in both communities as on other days, although I must admit there was a bit more barracking than usual on this particular day. As I began to make my way along the Falls Road there were about five or six voices all shouting at me at the same time. What they were shouting was not worth responding to and is not worth printing in full. I did not look around to see who they were or where they were standing, but in the words of T. D. Jakes, 'I just kept on walking'. I heard them call out my name as they shouted, 'Hey, McKee! Away back to the Shankill!' but I just kept on walking. Again I was called a header, with a few added expletives, but I just kept on walking. I felt somewhat anxious, but I was determined to win through, and so I just kept on walking as their voices became more distant with every step I took.

Later, as I walked along the Springfield Road, a car came close to me from behind. As it picked up speed the driver put his fist into the air through his open window and shouted loudly, 'Up the Re' Ra!' I turned to Denis, who was walking on the pavement nearby, and told him what the guy had shouted. Denis said, 'That means the Real IRA,' which of course I already knew! I said to Denis, 'Well, they can love me or hate me, but they can't ignore me, and they can't ignore the cross!'

Soon after this another two young men in their late teens began to shout at me. I did not quite make out what they were shouting, but I knew it was not worth asking them to repeat it, but this time I did stop and ask them if they wanted to talk. They shook their heads, indicating a clear 'no'. So I told them that God loved them and that Jesus died for them. At this point they dropped their heads as if embarrassed, and then they kept on walking.

Notwithstanding the above encounters, there were many positive responses in both communities. Horns were sounding, hands were waving and hats were taken off as a sign of respect. Some of the Catholics actually 'blessed' themselves at the sight of the cross. Others spoke words of encouragement. At one point Denis encouraged me by saying, 'Jack, the positive far outweighs the negative.' I responded, 'You're right, Denis, but you know if it was the other way round, we would still be doing this.'

Heads were turned and eyes were lifted

The messages of support just kept coming in, and man was I thankful! When an athlete enters a race, he or she does not do so with any thought of giving up before the finish. However, there are certain points in the race where the athlete just needs to hear someone shout words of encouragement, telling them to hang in there or to keep going.

This is what the messages of support meant to me. They were like shouts from the terraces that helped keep me focused on the need to finish the course. Let me make it clear, however, that the thought of giving up had never entered my mind, no matter what the weather and no matter what the response from others. I had long since learned to live by not fearing what men can do to the body. Solomon said, 'Fear of man will prove to be a snare' (Prov 29:25), but he also said, 'The fear of the Lord is the beginning of wisdom' (Prov 9:10).

Day 12 was another good day, and without the barracking of the previous day. One of the first people to approach me was a priest on the Falls Road. He said to me, 'How's it going?' I said, 'Fine thanks.' He then asked, 'Are you getting any hassle from anyone?' I said (with tongue in cheek), 'No, everyone's great.' Now I must admit that I did not feel it was confession time, nor did I feel that I wanted to get any of his parishioners into trouble! Anyway, up to that moment and on that day, everyone *was* great, so I was not telling lies! He wished me well, we shook hands and I kept on walking.

Further up the Falls Road a Catholic woman had been waiting to greet me. She had been standing talking with Denis on the pavement. She said she had heard what I was doing and wanted to walk with me for a while. She then walked alongside Denis and finally stopped off at a spot along the Springfield Road. It was a bold gesture for this woman from the Falls Road to walk alongside this cross-carrying pastor from the Shankill Road, but it was much appreciated on my part.

Once again horns were sounding and hands were waving. A number of drivers took the time to stop and politely ask me what I was doing. So I took the opportunity to briefly explain and also to tell them that God loved them. Their response was often accompanied by a look of bewilderment, but was always positive. I was conscious that from the priest in the car to the woman on the pavement, and to all who spoke or just waved at me, heads were turned and eyes were lifted to focus on the cross. People were so used to seeing the gun and its effects, but they were now seeing the cross as a symbol that represented love, forgiveness and reconciliation.

The cross does the talking

The following day (Day 13), I was joined by Pastor Mark Armstrong, Assistant Pastor at New Life, and again by Denis. They each took their place on the pavement on either side of me. I had no sooner begun my walk along the Falls Road when someone shouted from a car, 'Well done, Jack! Keep it going!' Soon someone shouted from another car, this time a woman, 'Bless you, brother. We're all praying for you.' Then there was the usual sounding of horns and hand waves.

A minibus carrying a number of American tourists had stopped outside the Sinn Fein/IRA offices. Several of them took photographs as I walked by with the cross. They waved and expressed a number of encouraging comments. Later, when I was heading back to the Shankill, I saw the same minibus waiting for me. The driver had obviously wanted them to see that I was walking on both sides of the dividing wall. They took some more photographs, only this time on the Shankill Road, and then they gave a few more hand waves before driving off.

As I walked along the Shankill Road a taxi driver stopped me. I don't know if he was enquiring for himself or for his passengers, but he said to me, 'Why are you carrying the cross?' I replied, 'I'm doing this walk along the Falls Road and the Shankill Road because I want people to know that no matter who they are or what they are, God loves them and Jesus died for them.' He said, 'Are you looking to preach to them?' I said, 'No, I do the walking and the cross does the talking!'

As I began to walk on, it was as if the Holy Spirit whispered into my ear, 'Jack, you're preaching to more people during this walk than you would normally preach to during an entire year.' You see, the foolishness of preaching means much more than imposing a 30- to 40-minute sermon on people. It's got more to do with our actions than our words, and our willingness to take the opportunities to be witnesses of the truth. Sometimes you don't need a sermon, but you do need a cross. The old adage states, 'Actions speak louder than words.' I think this also means sermons, although I'm not knocking sermons, for these are a great way of communicating the gospel. Besides, I'm still preaching sermons every week, and good ones at that! However, proclaiming the gospel is not simply about preaching the word; it is more about living the word. Paul talked about the foolishness of preaching (1 Cor 1:21), but he lived a life that backed up his sermonizing and even reminded the Corinthians that they were also epistles of Christ, who are known and read of all men (see 2 Cor 3:1–3), and this is what we are.

A question on violence

During these days of the Cross Walk a number of people from the USA emailed and asked about the violence in Northern Ireland. I think they were simply wondering if the Cross Walk had been having any kind of impact in this area. I have to say that things were generally much quieter during that time, although there was barely a night that went by without someone being shot or severely beaten by terrorists.

For example, at that time the IRA had beaten a young Catholic man in the Ardoyne area of north Belfast. They then proceeded to shoot him in both hands and both ankles as punishment for 'crimes' that they had judged him to be guilty of. Likewise, another young man, this time a Protestant, was badly beaten in Carrickfergus by Loyalists, who then proceeded to shoot him in the leg.

I would love to be able to say that the Cross Walk had the effect of reducing violence within our community, and maybe it did to some extent, but one thing I do know is that the cross was lifted not in the absence of violence, but in the midst of violence as a much more powerful message than that of the gun. For the gun, as an instrument of conflict, sends out a message on the weakness of hate. But the cross, as an instrument of peace, sends out a message on the strength of love.

Under the watchful eyes of the law

By the time I had started my walk on the second Sunday morning, all 'good Christians' were already in church. Most others, who do not generally attend church, were merely resting at home, as Sunday is normally a rest day in Northern Ireland, except for those, like pastors, who are unfortunate enough to have to work, or those who manage to find an open pub, even if it is through a side door!

However, there were still enough people on the streets of the Falls and Shankill Roads, so the day would certainly not be wasted. While walking along the Springfield Road a Catholic man in his late twenties, with two girls beside him, walked to the centre of the road towards me. Under the watchful eye of police officers in the look-out post above the gate of the Springfield Road police station, the young man said to me, 'Hey Pastor, what does "JOHN 3:16" mean?' Wow! Here was this guy, with a girl virtually on each arm and the police looking on, and he wanted to know what John 3:16 meant!

Well, as you can imagine, I again took the opportunity to explain that John 3:16 was a verse in the Bible and then to quote that verse and explain what it meant to both him and the two girls who were listening in. Having listened to me, the young man responded, 'Those are very nice sentiments!' He then thanked me and wished me well, and we began to walk our separate ways, but not before shaking hands. I turned to Denis, who was standing nearby, and said, 'You know, Denis, that one thing on its own has made the walk today worthwhile.' This was already a good Sunday, and I hadn't even got to church yet!

Soon after this, three young lads followed us on their mountain bikes. They had a look of bewilderment on their faces as they stared at me and at the cross with the inscription 'JOHN 3:16'. I greeted them a couple of times, but they wouldn't speak. It seemed they just wanted to look at what they saw as a strange sight of a man carrying a cross in the middle of the road. At least they didn't call me a header!

They followed me until I got to Lanark Way, and then they stopped. They stopped because they knew that beyond the security gate in the wall was 'the other side'. In all probability they had never been to 'the other side'. May God help us to break down the barriers!

Chapter Nine

AGAINST ALL ELEMENTS

Day 15 and I was still being encouraged by the positive responses of people in both communities. They are divided against each other by a concrete wall and by years of sectarianism, yet in some strange way they (that is, most people) were united in their attitude towards and a respect for the cross.

As I began to walk along the Falls Road a car pulled up alongside me. The driver spoke and said, 'Well done, Pastor! I know what you're trying to do here.' He went on to say, 'Someday before you finish I plan to park the car and get out and walk with you for a bit.' I thanked him for his words of encouragement and shook hands with him before he drove on. I never did see him again, but the brief encounter was one among many that remained with me for some time.

The life scared out of me!

Shortly after this I could hear the rumbling of a huge truck coming from behind me. The driver did not slow down. In fact it seemed he came as close to me as he dared and then let out an amazing blast of the truck's trumpet horn. Man, I don't mind telling you, it scared the life out of me! It brought home to me again just how dangerous it is to walk along the centre of the road at any time, never mind while carrying a seven-foot cross!

Again there were the usual, but now expected, exchanges and greetings. While walking along Lanark Way I was joined by a man who attended a church I had pastored for ten years. He put his arm around my shoulder and walked with me for a while. He said, 'Pastor, we've all heard what you're doing, and I want you to know that we're all praying for you.' He went on to say, 'You know, when I first heard what you were doing, I began to cry before the Lord. This is touching a lot of people, and you gotta keep it up.' I thanked him and assured him that I would indeed complete the 40-Day Walk. I encouraged him to keep on praying and explained how much it helped just to know that others were praying for me during those days.

Almost without incident

The following day passed by without much incident. In fact the only thing that seemed noteworthy was some guy walking along the centre of the road while carrying a seven-foot wooden cross against the wind, and that was me! There was much the same, but very welcome hand waves and verbal greetings from pedestrians and motorists. Hardly a taxi driver on the Falls Road passed by without waving, and it was much the same on the Shankill Road.

It was only when I had actually finished the walk and moved off the road to go back into the church that two men approached me. They had been walking on the pavement parallel with me for a while along the Shankill Road. One of them pointed to the inscription 'JOHN 3:16' on the cross and asked me what it meant. This was the first person to ask me this question on the Shankill Road.

As I had done so many times already on the Falls Road, I was happy to share John 3:16 with this man and his friend and then to explain what it meant – not only for the world, but for him and his friend as individuals. He told me he would like to come to church, so I gave him the invitation. He said he would hopefully see me on Sunday. He did keep his word and came along to church the following Sunday. He also made a commitment to follow Christ. The man sadly has an alcohol problem, and although this is hindering his development as a Christian, he is still maintaining contact with us at New Life.

God was in the wind

As I prepared myself to begin the walk on Day 17 I was again concerned about the weather. This day seemed to be the worst so far! It was not the wettest or the snowiest, but was certainly the stormiest. Again I prayed for the strength of Samson and the wisdom of Solomon. During all other days I had managed to do what Samson would have done and to push on regardless of the wind, but today the wisdom of Solomon had to take precedence. I managed to walk the first few hundred yards while carrying the cross high on my chest, but even that was a battle.

When I began to walk along the Falls Road I was seriously hampered, not by the occasional gusts of wind, but by a constant strong wind that literally held me to the spot and prevented me from moving forward. Sometimes the wind became so strong that it even managed to move me backwards. I knew it would be too dangerous, not to mention foolish, to walk the centre of the road or to carry the cross in my normal way, so I reluctantly lifted it down, placed it over my shoulder, and 'kept on walking'. I finally decided to move off the centre of the road and for the first time to walk along the pavement for the duration of the walk or at least until the wind subsided.

This gave me a whole new experience, for now I was able to make good eye contact with people as we passed by on the pavement. The amazing thing was that motorists, including taxi drivers, still waved as they drove past. Many pedestrians greeted me and commented on the windy conditions. It seemed that my presence in the Falls community was not only accepted, but actually expected! It appeared that some were actually looking for the pastor with the cross from the Shankill. They knew I was normally walking through their community between 11 a.m. and 12 noon each day, and whether I was on the road or the pavement didn't seem to matter to them. I was welcome to walk the road and just as welcome to walk alongside them on the pavement.

While walking down the Shankill Road, still on the pavement as the strong winds had not abated, I was stopped by a man who asked, 'What are you doing it for?' He went on to say, 'I work in the estate agents and we have been watching you walk down the road with the cross every day for the past couple of weeks, and we've been wondering why you're doing it.' I then took time to explain John 3:16 and the reason behind the Cross Walk.

He thanked me and wished me well, then headed back to his office, where he would no doubt explain to his friends the reason why I was doing the Cross Walk. I soon realized that this, along with other opportunities, was only made possible because of the wind, and that what the devil may have meant as a hindrance, God used for good.

Sometimes we have to lay the cross down

The next day I was delighted to see that the sun was shining and the wind had abated. I was back on the road at 11 a.m. and walking through the first security gate of the dividing wall between the Shankill and the Falls communities. No sooner had I begun to walk along the Falls Road when I heard someone shout, 'Hey!' I looked round and there was a young man who had pulled up in his car by the side of the road. He shouted to me, 'What are you doing that for?' So I shouted back, 'Give me a few minutes of your time and I'll explain.' He agreed, so I walked over to the car. As I got closer I could see more clearly that this was a young man in his early twenties. I could also see that he had a fresh looking black eye. He was obviously quite moved as I explained the reason behind the walk and then went on to explain John 3:16. Before he left he enquired as to the whereabouts of our church and said he would come along some night.

His final words to me before he drove off were, 'Watch yourself on the Falls. I know what they're like. I live there!' Then off he went. Ten minutes later, as I walked further along the Falls Road, the same young man came driving down the road towards me. He had obviously driven around the block to drive past me for one more look. He sounded his horn and gave me a wave as he drove by. My heart went out to him, but unfortunately I have not seen him since.

On I walked to the usual greetings that I had become accustomed to. Soon I was walking back down the Shankill Road. I was almost finished when I spoke to an elderly man I had known for 20 years. I asked him how he was doing. He put his hand to his chest and said, 'Not well, Jack. I need to go home.' Jimmy was quite a few miles from home. He walks everywhere he goes, and by the look of him he would not make it back home that day.

So I lifted the cross down, and then took him by the arm and sat him on a seat inside the local KFC. I asked one of the young women who worked in KFC to look after him while I went for my car. When I went back outside, there was my superintendent, Pastor Eric McComb. He had been driving up the Shankill Road looking for me for the purpose of giving some moral support. I explained to him what had happened with the elderly man, and he immediately offered to take him home in his car.

After I got Jimmy settled into Pastor Eric's car, I proceeded to complete the last 100 yards of the walk. The lesson I learned from this is that sometimes we must be willing to lay down the cross and do something practical or, as James put it, 'Faith without works is dead.'

The following day (Day 19) was virtually uneventful. In fact the only thing that seemed eventful about the day was the walk itself! In comparison to previous days, this was a quiet day. No one even barracked me! I thought this might happen when I got to the Springfield Road, where I saw five young men standing outside a bakery shop eating cakes (wee buns!). They seemed to be bracing themselves for my arrival. However, when I got to them they just stood there and looked at me. One of them gave me a 'thumbs up' and smiled with a suggestion of approval!

A young woman prays

Day 20 was a major milestone, because this was halfway in the 40-Day Cross Walk. However, let me take a step back if I may! The previous night, at exactly 20 minutes after midnight, my telephone rang. A young woman was crying on the other end of the line. Christine was obviously well intoxicated, but she told me that for the past three weeks she had kept thinking about church. Her father was with her at the time and was quite concerned about her, so I got into the car and drove to their home.

Christine shared with me that three weeks earlier, at 2.30 on a Saturday morning, she was standing outside a police station in the Shankill community, crying to the police officer on duty and telling him she needed to get to a church. Knowing that no church would be open at 2.30 in the morning, the police officer got her a lift home in one of the patrol cars.

As she sat holding my hand and weeping, she went on to tell me that she would often watch me walking along the Shankill carrying the cross. She said, 'I felt sorry for you, Jackie, and I prayed that God would bless you when you were walking past me.' As she sat and cried, still holding my hand, I said, 'What is it you want, Christine?' She responded, 'I want Jesus. I want to get saved.' So, in the early hours of the morning, I had the joy of leading her in a prayer to receive Jesus as her Lord and Saviour. She immediately went to the phone and called her sister, who is on our worship team at New Life Fellowship.

After this, it was back to bed for a few hours and then up again to commence Day 20 of the Cross Walk. This was to be a lively day and was to make up for the quietness of the previous day. It seemed that more and more people wanted to pass on their greetings and wish me well.

One of the first things I was called on to do was to step off the road for a while and talk with a group of Americans who were standing outside the Sinn Fein office on the Falls Road. They were keen to know what I was doing. As we stood there talking, Martin Meehan pulled up in his car and went into the Sinn Fein office. I think he got a good glimpse of the cross and I hope that in some way he got the message. (You may not know who he is, but he is worth mentioning, or some would say 'worth ignoring'.)

As I walked along the Springfield Road a van driver told me I would not get through Lanark Way as the security gates were closed. I thought he was joking, but no, he was right. The gates were closed. However, I could see there was a police Land Rover parked in front of the gates. So with the cross still held high I continued to walk towards the police, who for some reason were guarding the gates.

I stopped and enquired as to why the gates were closed. They explained that maintenance work was being carried out, but that I could walk on through! Wow! Well, thank you, Jesus! I have since been looking out for the man in the van to let him know that if the Red Sea could not stop Moses, then no security gate was big enough to stop Pastor Jack!

Weather-beaten, but not defeated

The following day, all of the weather forecast services were warning of serious weather conditions, and they were right. Within the first five minutes of the walk I was completely soaked through and weather-beaten. At one point I almost took off like a kite!

However, before setting off on the walk, two of the Americans I had been speaking to the previous day turned up at the church and asked if they could walk with me. I was happy for them to do so as long as they walked on the pavement. It was towards the end of this first section that the weather was so boisterous that I almost lost it! My two new friends came to my rescue and helped me take the cross down. We then moved to the pavement, where Denis soon met with us. He told me he had got it on good authority that the weather would clear up in five minutes! He was absolutely correct, and soon I was back to the centre of the road with the cross again being lifted high.

A man by the name of Joe came out from beyond the gates of the convent where a nun had approached me two weeks earlier and offered me a drink. He greeted me and wished me well. He also invited me in for tea and something to eat, but I had to decline. As we talked together someone started to barrack me from a car. Joe said, 'That's the old devil, Jack. He doesn't like what you're doing.'

As I continued the walk I noticed a very heavy security presence and thought there must be something wrong or something was happening. I mentioned this to Denis, and he said, 'Yes, Jack. Did you not see the men with the banners and flags down near the Sinn Fein office? They seemed to be holding some kind of ceremony.' I said to Denis, 'It's as well I didn't see them, otherwise I would have been tempted to go and stand beside them with the cross!' However, I knew that although I had not seen them, they certainly would have seen me walking past with the cross.

When I got to Lanark Way a photographer from the *Irish News* was waiting for me. This is one of the main papers in Northern Ireland and is read mainly by Catholics. I thought to myself, 'Praise God! This paper will carry the story of the Cross Walk in the coming week.' I knew it was important, not for any personal reasons, but so that the message of the cross would be presented to a wider audience and that the reason behind the walk would be more fully explained. Soon it was back down the Shankill and back at church for our first service of the day.

Chapter Ten

MIGHTIER THAN THE GUN

Someone once said, 'The word is mightier than the pen.' However, I would want to add, 'The cross is mightier than the gun.' The more the walk continued, the more I appreciated those who had stayed with me for the long haul in terms of prayer and messages of encouragement. These continued to make me feel that this was not the walk of a lone ranger, but one that represented the hopes and prayers of many. It made me feel that my failure would be their failure, but that my success would be their success.

Once again there was an excellent response in both the Falls and Shankill communities. I began to get to know the regulars – those who would normally be around between 11 a.m. and midday. Probably the most notable thing about this day (Day 22) was the hand waves I received from two police officers travelling in a Land Rover. On Day 1 I was told by the police to get off the road, but today they were waving at me! This made me think that even the law must give way, not only to Grace, but also to the cross!

The following day (Day 23) I was approached by four

Americans who had heard about the Cross Walk. They wanted to know more about what I was doing, not just in carrying the cross, but also in my daily work within the community. We walked and talked for a while, but soon they had to move to the pavement. At the end of the walk they explained how much it had affected their lives to walk and talk with me and to see something of what I was doing in Belfast.

During the walk, there was much of the same of previous days. More police officers joined in the waving, which confirmed that my presence on the road with the cross was well accepted at many levels. I knew that as long as I kept myself safe from the oncoming traffic, and as long as I did not make things difficult for the motorists, my presence would be tolerated for the duration of the 40 days. However, the police did not speak for the entire community, and sooner or later some of those who had not yet done so would let me know of their feelings.

The most notable thing about this day was a meeting I had with five young people in their mid to late teens. They stopped me, right underneath a sangar (a look-out post) at the front of the police station on the Springfield Road. One of them approached me and said, 'Hey mister, what are you doing?' When I told them I was carrying the cross for 40 days around the Shankill and Falls communities one of them said, 'Aye right! So ya go onto the Shankill with that, do ya?' He had a look of total disbelief, but was further amazed when I told him that I was actually from the Shankill!

One of them then said, 'Well, why are you doing this?' Again I was delighted to take the opportunity to explain and to let them know that God loves them and that Jesus died for them as much as for anyone else. They thanked me and moved on. Normally when these young men thought of people from the Shankill they would picture men pointing guns at them, yet here was someone from the Shankill who didn't have a gun, but a cross. Once again the cross was presented as an object with a positive message and was lifted up as something that is greater and mightier than the gun.

Promoted down under

I continued daily to check my emails before I left home and was always encouraged by the many messages of support from across the world. Some would write to bid me 'good morning' or even 'top o' the mornin', Jack', and to wish me well for the day. Others would send a 'thought for the day' or a prayer to help me on my way. One such message was from a pastor friend, Darryl Stott, in Australia. He told me how he had done a radio interview during which he had mentioned to the audience what I had been doing in Belfast. I had always believed that the Cross Walk would impact more people than I could ever imagine, and this was further evidence of the validity of this belief. The Cross Walk was now being promoted 'down under', and by this I mean Australia. Yet I wondered if another 'down under' was taking note! I think it was, as will soon become evident.

Towards the end of the walk on Day 24 I was stopped by two men who asked what 'John 3:16' was all about. One of them showed some knowledge of the verse, but when he spoke it was obvious by his accent that he was English. Then the second person spoke and it was immediately apparent that he was from Australia – not because he swore, but because his Aussie accent was so clear.

After having spoken for a while, the Australian asked if he could have his photograph taken alongside me holding the cross.

I happily obliged as his friend took the photograph. I also shared with them about the message I had received from Australia that very day and remarked on the impact the Cross Walk was obviously making, not only in Northern Ireland, but also in other parts of the world.

This had been another incredible day of opportunity, proving that not everyone in Northern Ireland was blinded by sectarian or religious bigotry. For example, a man shouted a greeting from his car while I was walking along the Falls Road. He then turned his car into the Springfield Road, where he parked and sat waiting for me to arrive. He wanted to talk with me. More on him in a moment.

Then there was another man. Like so many others, he also wanted to know what I was doing. For some reason he knew that Denis was with me, even though Denis had been walking along the footpath. He stopped Denis and told him he was an alcoholic. Denis spoke with the man as he walked, and shared with him how God could set him free from his addiction. Here was a Catholic man on the Falls Road walking alongside a Protestant man from the Shankill Road, and they were talking freely and friendly enough with each other.

After this, two young lads shouted to me, 'Hey mister! Why are you doing that?' I shouted back, 'Because I want everyone to know that God loves them.' Later, on the Springfield Road, three young men in their late teens or early twenties were looking at me quite strangely. When I greeted them from the centre of the road one of them nodded his head in the direction of the cross and said, 'What's that all about?' I replied, 'If you give me some of your time I'll come over and explain.' He answered, 'Aye, all right.' So I went and spoke to them and had one of the best times of sharing since the 40-Day Cross Walk began.

As we stood talking, a woman came out of a shop she owned and gave me a bottle of water. Another woman came out of another shop and asked me why I was walking with the cross. When I explained and shared John 3:16 with her, and how people can be sure of heaven, she responded, 'Well, everyone to their own opinion!' I then replied, 'Yes, everyone has their own opinion. That's why I'm sharing John 3:16, because that explains God's opinion!' She smiled as she got into her car and drove off.

When I then moved to the centre of the road I was called to by the same man who had shouted to me from his car on the Falls Road earlier (I mentioned him above). He had driven to the Springfield Road to talk with me. It turned out that this was the same man who had spoken to me on Day 3, when he asked if things were quiet enough for me. He now wanted to know how things had been going for me during the walk.

After explaining about the good reception I had been receiving and that many times people had asked what 'JOHN 3:16' means, he then said to me, 'Well, between you and me, what does it mean?' Wow! So I stood with him for a while and went through John 3:16 and told him how much God loves him. Having chatted for a while, he wished me well and then drove back towards the Falls Road. I have not seen him since.

Just one more story for this day: I was stopped again on Lanark Way as I made my way towards the Shankill Road. This time it was a young Protestant man (of 18), who also wanted to know what 'JOHN 3:16' was all about. I moved to the pavement, where I spent some time explaining to this young man the content and meaning of John 3:16. I could see that his eyes were glazed and that he was on something. He then told me his name was David and that the only thing he lived for was dope. I responded to him by saying, 'You know, David, there was a young man in the Bible called David and God used him to defeat a giant.' I then said, 'God is still looking for young men like you to destroy some giants in this country, but the first thing you must defeat is the dope that is seeking to destroy you.'

When I had finished speaking with him I invited him to New Life and told him I would be praying for him. My concern was that if God did not get a hold of this young man, the terrorists would (if they had not already done so). The Shankill and the Falls Roads do not need more young men to take up the gun, but rather to take up the cross and to stand for a greater cause than that of sectarian religion or politics.

Promoted in the USA

Day 25 started with the knowledge that the Cross Walk was also being promoted in the USA. Many of my American friends were able to tune in to KKLA as Warren Duffy gave me an awesome introduction followed by an excellent interview that lasted 15 minutes. This was informing people across southern California and other parts of the USA about the Cross Walk and its impact. I would like to thank Warren Duffy and Natasha at KKLA for giving me this amazing opportunity and for encouraging others to pray for the success of the walk.

This was followed by several interviews on Prime Time America, Moody Broadcasting in Chicago. I would therefore also like to thank Greg Wheatley, the program host, and Dave Oseland, the senior producer, for staying in touch with me and for giving me the opportunity to speak to a wider American audience. As a result of these I received numerous emails from people who heard about the Cross Walk and about the work of

New Life Ministries Ireland for the first time. Some of these have continued to remain in contact.

Things turn ugly

Every day of the walk seemed to be different. Day 25 started as most other days, with hand waves and greetings. It began with one man walking right up to me on the Falls Road. He shook my hand and wished me well. But immediately after this things turned ugly. I saw reactions that day that I had not seen during the previous 24 days. More people shouted obscenities at me and swore at me than all the previous days put together.

I remember literally feeling the presence of an evil force as some were shouting at me to go back to the Shankill. However, I continued to walk without reacting against the negative comments. In fact I prayed as I walked, and as I did so the heaviness in the atmosphere began to lift. Once again I began to feel at ease as I walked between the trucks and the buses! In spite of the bombardment of verbal abuse it seemed that many more people, both motorists and pedestrians alike, began to do their best to encourage me. Theirs were the faces I chose to see and theirs were the voices I chose to hear.

As the atmosphere continued to improve I was approached by another man. He was not local, nor was he American or Australian. In fact he was a German named Roland. He was keen to know why I was walking with the cross. I explained it was my desire to promote the message that God loves everyone equally, whether it's the Protestants on the Shankill Road or the Catholics on the Falls Road.

I finished off by telling him that God also loves Germans. This brought a welcome smile to his face, after which he continued to walk alongside Denis on the pavement until we got back to the Shankill. So the previous day it was an Aussie and an Englishman, the day before that it was Americans, and now it was the Germans. You see, 'God so loved *the World*'. The cross embraces all nationalities and all cultures.

The first major challenges

The following day, Day 26, started off well. It seemed to be much improved from the previous day. Once again many responded positively as I continued the walk through both communities. More and more people were participating in hand waving and positive verbal greetings. However, I reminded myself of the words of Jesus when He said, 'Woe to you when all men speak well of you' (Lk 6:26), and then again when He said, 'If the world hates you, keep in mind that it hated me first' (Jn 15:18). This made me realize that if the Cross Walk really was making an impact the response would not simply be positive, but in fact a hornets' nest would be stirred.

Of course, we should not go out of our way to cause people to speak ill of us or to hate us, but we must acknowledge that sometimes just standing for what's right is enough to draw negative responses. I was always thankful for the positive responses and for the warm reception I received in both communities, yet I somehow began to feel that in the run up to Day 40 the atmosphere might well change for the worse. This was not a defeatist attitude on my part, but was an acknowledgement of the fact that there were forces afoot that would try to prevent me from fulfilling this challenge.

There was further evidence of this again on Day 26, when I faced two major confrontations. The first was when a car pulled out of a shopping area on the Springfield Road with four men on board. The driver, a Catholic man, yelled out, 'Hey Jack! How's Marty doing?' At first I did not know who he was talking about, but then he shouted, 'Tell the b*** the IRA have not gone away.' It was then it dawned on me that he was talking about Martin McGartland, whom the IRA had tried to kill and whom I had helped as recorded in my first book *Through Terror and Adversity*.

When I realized he was talking about Martin McGartland I immediately shouted back, 'I don't where he is. I haven't spoken to him in ages!' He laughed and drove off while I continued with my walk, knowing that some in this community knew me better than others and perhaps better than I thought! But who were they? Who was he? Well, the fact is I did not know who he was, but I was left in no doubt who he represented.

Immediately following this encounter there were another two men walking past me on the Springfield Road. One of them looked at me with hatred blazing from his eyes. Then with anger in his voice he screamed at me, 'Away back to the Shankill, ya Protestant b***.' I looked straight into his eyes and said, 'God bless you, my friend.' He repeated the above and I responded, 'God bless you.' He came back at me for a third time with the same expletive, and again I responded as before.

This was repeated about seven times in total. It appeared he wanted to come into the centre of the road and rip the cross out of my hands, or maybe it was my head he wanted to rip off my shoulders. However, it was obvious there was something stopping him from taking action against me, and I'm not simply talking about the Holy Spirit! It was becoming more apparent with each passing day that he, and others like him, was under orders not to harm me, much as he apparently wanted to.

He was wearing a woollen hat with the colours of the Irish

flag, which are green, white and orange. The green represents the Catholic community in Ireland, the orange represents the Protestant community in Ireland (Northern Ireland and the Republic of Ireland), and the white is a symbol of peace between both communities. Yet here was a man with these colours on his head, calling me a 'Protestant b***!'

Many on the street were listening to his ranting, and I am quite sure they were disgusted as he disgraced the colours of the Irish flag that covered his head. I thank God that I did not disgrace the cross, for while he spoke hatred, I responded by speaking love.

This was followed by many encouraging responses from people who appreciated what I was doing. Some shouted, 'Keep it up, Pastor!' Perhaps the most encouraging thing during this day was a driver in a black taxi on the Falls Road, who shouted, 'God bless you, Pastor.' His greeting, added to that of others, meant a lot to me and again helped to spur me on. Shortly after this I was offered money from a truck driver. I explained that I was not collecting money, but I simply wanted to share the message of God's love with the people on either side of the wall. He gave me the strangest look and then drove on. I then walked on regardless towards the Shankill Road and back to New Life Fellowship church.

The following day (Day 27) was much quieter than the previous two days. The very atmosphere seemed much more favourable. More and more people were joining in to make me feel welcome on both the Falls Road and the Shankill Road. They would speak to me from the pavement or from cars, with many using my first name as if they really knew me! However, my desire was and is that they might come to know Christ.

I had almost finished my walk when five young men

approached me at the bottom of the Shankill Road. They were interested in what I was doing. All of them were wearing red, white and blue scarves and hats, and were on their way to a soccer match. Their colours quite clearly identified them as Protestants, as these are the British colours to which the Protestants give allegiance.

They could not believe that I had actually walked along the Falls Road or that I had been allowed to do so by the Catholics who lived there. They went on to the game to cheer their team and their heroes, but not before they heard of the world's greatest hero, who had laid down His life both for them and for their Catholic neighbours.

Chapter Eleven

THE CROSS ON ST PATRICK'S DAY

When I had first set out on this 40-Day Cross Walk I had not even considered that St Patrick's Day would be one of those days, but this was it – Day 28. This was St Patrick's Day in Ireland (Northern and Southern), which of course was also being celebrated in other parts of the world, especially in the USA, where more people claim to be Irish than those who actually live in Ireland.

As I walked along the same route I had taken for the previous 27 days I saw plenty of green, white and orange décor; I saw shamrocks and leprechauns; I saw decorated pubs and decorated taxis, and I saw people dressed for this festive anniversary to commemorate Ireland's most famous Welsh-born (or some say Scottish-born) saint. However, I saw nothing that represented the Christian faith that St Patrick had faithfully and passionately promoted in Ireland some 1,600 years ago.

As I continued with my walk, once again holding the cross aloft, I felt I heard the Lord speak to my heart. As if to encourage me He said, 'If Patrick were alive in Ireland today, he would be walking along the streets beside you and would also be carrying a cross.' This made me feel so warm inside and so honoured to be the only person walking with a cross on the Falls Road and the Shankill Road on St Patrick's Day.

However, it was disappointing to see that in the midst of the St Patrick's Day celebrations in Belfast there was nothing to celebrate what he had preached or what he truly believed. One young woman, wearing her St Patrick's Day T-shirt, shouted to me, 'Hey mister! You're a header.' I then thought to myself at that very moment, 'How sad that on St Patrick's Day in Ireland, the man who carries a cross is the one considered to be a header!' And I wondered what they really would have thought of Patrick!

However, having said this, more and more people greeted me from the pavement and wished me well, some lifting their pints of beer in my direction in a posture of affirmation and cheer. I then passed a group of over 20 men, with Denis on the pavement having to walk right through the middle of them. Initially both of us felt there was going to be some hostility, but when I shouted over and greeted them with, 'Have a good day, men! Enjoy your St Patrick's Day!' they responded in kind and were quite friendly towards us. They spoke to Denis and wished him well. I could see that Denis was quite relieved to say the least!

Just before getting to the Springfield Road police station there was quite a loud explosion. It sounded as if a blast bomb had been thrown, although it turned out to be a controlled explosion carried out by British soldiers on a suspicious device nearby. It made Denis and me look round immediately at each other and question where it might have been, but we knew it was close. Within moments I had to step off the road and onto the pavement, as I could hear the sound of emergency vehicles coming towards me on the Springfield Road. As I got to the pavement two fire engines sped past making their way to the scene of the explosion.

As I stood on the pavement a man approached me and asked, 'Why are you carrying the cross?' Once again I explained John 3:16 and the reason behind the walk. He told me he was aware of what I was doing, but wanted to know more about the why. I was delighted to chat with him and briefly explain the gospel to him. We gave him a little card with John 3:16 and its explanation on it. We wished each other well and then moved on. He went back towards the Falls Road and I went back to the centre of the road with the cross. Soon I was back at church for our Sunday morning service on this St Patrick's Day.

Patrick was an early Christian pioneer who is credited for having introduced the message of the cross to Ireland, although Christianity had in fact spread to Ireland before Patrick ever got to these shores during the fifth century AD. However, someone more sinister and with a darker agenda introduced the gun as a means of achieving religious and political objectives, and with the erroneous belief, still prevalent among some in Ireland today, that the end justifies the means.

Subsequently, somewhere down the historical road someone ironically and sadistically denigrated the greatest symbol of God's love by creating an unholy alliance with the greatest symbol of man's hatred. This has resulted in the cross and the gun often being partnered in Ireland's religious and political conflicts, and often with dire and tragic consequences. Patrick would be disgusted at such a corrupt partnership.

St Patrick's Day is gone, diabolos comes out!

At the end of Day 29 I sent out the following email report: 'I will not comment on today other than to ask for your prayers for the remainder of this 40-Day Walk.' I went on to write, 'I have a feeling that the remaining 11 days are going to seem long.' I then expressed my appreciation to the people of the Shankill Road and also to the people of the Falls Road for their openness in receiving me. At that time I could not write what I am about to write now as I did not want to jeopardize the remaining two weeks of the walk.

What happened was that a very serious and threatening situation developed as I moved to the middle of the Falls Road beside the Divis Street flats. For several days I had noticed two and sometimes three men watching me from one of the flats. At times they seemed to be videoing me as I walked past with the cross. This had concerned me, although it did not cause me to fear.

On Day 29 two others from New Life Fellowship (Pastor Mark Armstrong and Sam Anderson) had come along with me for the purpose of handing out cards that explained the reason behind the Cross Walk. As we walked towards Divis Street and the Falls Road I had been joking with them about those who had been watching me from the window of one of the flats. When we got to Divis Street, sure enough there they were looking through the same window.

However, I noticed them suddenly withdraw from the window and very soon they were coming through the front door of the flats. One of them made his way across the road and came right up to me in the centre of the road. A very serious and threatening confrontation ensued. During this confrontation it became quite apparent as to who was in charge of 'the turf' on the Falls Road! The person who confronted us was in fact a senior member or a local commander of the IRA in that area.

To be fair, his problem was not so much with me walking with the cross, but rather the fact that there were two other people walking alongside me, albeit they were on the footpath! The atmosphere became extremely tense as he threatened to punch the heads off Pastor Mark and Sam. We understood quite rapidly that he was not just spouting off at the mouth. This guy was serious, and looked strong enough and mad enough to carry out his threats.

As he was breathing out his threats, using his extensive range of expletives and demanding that Mark and Sam go back to the Shankill from where they came, another Catholic man, who had greeted us on a previous day, saw what was happening and came to our assistance. But the local IRA commander (I'm assuming that's what he was) quickly turned on the other Catholic man and said, 'If you open your 'f***ing' mouth I'll dig the 'f***ing' head of you.' This caused our Good Samaritan friend to immediately freeze on the spot, and this was a clear signal to us concerning the position and the power that this person actually had within the Falls community.

As I was doing my best to 'negotiate' with him, but getting nowhere, another man came to the centre of the road with the intention of getting involved. He did not have the look of a deliverer. In fact I feared for him. I looked at the man who had been threatening and I looked at the man who had just joined in, and I thought to myself, 'If he opens his mouth, this guy will kill him.' However, it was the very opposite, and it soon became apparent that the man who had just joined us was in fact superior in rank to the man who had been spewing out threats.

This new guy finally took charge of the situation and, although still very tense, a compromise was finally reached where it was agreed that two people would be 'allowed' to walk with me, one on either footpath. However, I knew that their safety could not be guaranteed. I personally felt quite safe, but I feared for those who were with me.

So even though the compromise had been reached, after reflecting on what had happened it was agreed between us that I should complete the remainder of the 40 days on my own. Even Denis would have to wait for me as I returned through the security gates in Lanark Way and back to the Shankill community, rather than wait for me on the Falls Road as he had done in previous days.

My intention was never to cause offence or upset for anyone, although there are times when this cannot be avoided. Neither was it my intention to put people's lives at risk. I became quite concerned about Denis and his safety, as he would normally meet with me at the same place and at the same time every morning. Those who know something about our situation in Northern Ireland will know that this type of routine can be extremely dangerous.

So we completed Day 29 as we had started out, but the following day I was virtually on my own. I had started the walk along the Falls Road when I noticed two men keeping pace with me on the left-hand pavement. Further along the road I began to slow down, and as I did so I noticed the two men also slowing down, actually keeping pace with me. A little further up the road I noticed a TV camera crew who had been waiting for me. They filmed me as I walked past. It was at this point that the two men who had been keeping pace with me actually dropped off. They then just disappeared!

But having said all this, this was another great day. All the positive signs were back again. There were many people who were obviously delighted to see me back on the road, lifting the cross above the communities, above the dividing wall and above the gun. There was no doubt in my mind that God was using this to impact our communities. The people can stay away from church in their thousands, but they could not ignore the cross or its message that confronted them on a daily basis during those 40 days.

Due to the concerns of previous days, I felt I needed to assure those who were praying for me that I would complete the walk. I had no intention of giving up on the very thing that God had challenged me to do. However, I knew that I would not finish the task in my own strength, but in the strength and power of Almighty God and with the daily encouragement and prayers that came from so many brothers and sisters across the world.

God had spoken to us in New Life Fellowship several years earlier and had told us clearly that we would be a witness to our community, a witness to our nation and a witness to the nations. We never fully understood how this would happen, but the Cross Walk was a major development in this process and in the fulfilment of God's promise. We are still working this out in our continued obedience to God.

Countdown mode

Day 31 was another major milestone during the Cross Walk, for this was the commencement of countdown. I began this day with great expectation for the unfolding and fulfilment of God's purposes during the remaining nine days. However, I also set out on this day knowing that during the previous night serious riots had broken out between the Protestant and the Catholic communities in north Belfast. They had hurled petrol bombs and others missiles at each other. These riots came as a sad reminder that we still have a long way to go in Northern Ireland before we can truly say that the conflict is over.

As I walked from the Shankill Road and onto the Falls Road, I did so with an unusual feeling of apprehension, but with the confidence of God's presence and the prayers and support of many who were as much participants of this walk as I was. The first thing that happened, as I arrived at the kerbside on the Falls Road, was that the driver of a black taxi stopped his cab to allow me to walk in front of him and into the centre of the road. He waved me on and waited for me to get to the centre of the road before driving off. This was a good sign and was certainly much appreciated on my part.

I prayed for those who watched that they would not see me, but would see the cross and would be moved by its message. Soon I was greeting people on either side of the road and was responding to the hand waves and verbal greetings of motorists and pedestrians as they passed by. I noticed more and more people standing around in small groups. It was as if they were actually waiting for me. They greeted me with a friendly greeting and wished me well on my walk.

The following day began in much the same way, for no sooner had I walked through the first gate in the dividing wall than people began to welcome and greet me on the Falls Road. As I walked along the centre of the road there were again those who waved and those who spoke to me from the pavement. It was much the same along the Springfield Road, only here I did pick up a little bit of aggravation. In fact today was the first day of the walk I was called a 'Bible basher'!

Walking along Lanark Way towards the Shankill Road a woman stopped her car and asked me to pray for a young woman who was pregnant and being put under pressure to have an abortion. I assured her I would do so and that I would also have the church at New Life pray for her. Then as I walked down the Shankill Road and was responding to greetings and banter from many who knew me, I found myself walking faster than the traffic that was being held back due to a truck being double parked on a busy section of the road. However, like the traffic flowing in my direction, I was also stopping and starting several times until we passed the offending truck.

This gave me the opportunity to speak a little longer with motorists as I was keeping pace with them. One driver, whom I know quite well, asked me how my shoes were holding up. When I told him they were lasting quite well he responded, 'They would last twice as long on me.' It was then I remembered that he only had one leg! This is typical of Northern Ireland humour.

The following day was quite significant as a lot more prayer had gone up for this day than for any other day of the walk. This was due to a friend who felt within their spirit that Day 33 could present some very dangerous situations. As I began my walk it became obvious that the prayer support was kicking in. Even before I got out of Townsend Street and onto the Falls Road motorists were sounding their horns and people were waving at me from their cars.

There had been some excellent days of welcome, but this day outstripped them all. One taxi driver stopped his packed taxi alongside me on the Falls Road and said, 'Well done, Jack. Keep it up.' Others who were standing by the roadside also used my first name as they wished me well. A man who was crossing the road with his children said, 'Well done, mate. Keep it up.' Then I could see two women standing waiting for me, and with a sympathetic look they said, 'God bless you, son.'

As I passed an elderly woman who was carrying shopping bags she turned to me and said, 'Are you managing to hold out, son?' I responded, 'Yes, love, I'm doing OK thanks.' I felt that she was having more problems with her shopping than I was with the cross, but she was managing fine. Soon after this I was passing a building site where I had received some verbals in previous days, but on this day two men who were working on the site stood upright and nodded a nod of approval in my direction.

Then there was the man who had approached me on Day 3, and then again on Day 24. Once again he approached me today as I walked along the Falls Road. He stopped his car, causing others to stop behind him, and asked me how things had been going. After a brief response he wished me well for the rest of the walk and then drove on. Ten minutes later he stopped alongside me again, this time on the Springfield Road. He said, 'If I don't see you after today, I hope it goes well for you until you finish.' After I thanked him, he drove along the Springfield Road and out of sight. That was in fact the last time I did see him. But who knows!

The cross lights the way

Day 34 was the last Saturday of the 40-Day Cross Walk and although I was greeted in much the same way, yet there was a difference. As I walked along the centre of the road my attention was drawn to some motorists who were flashing their headlights as a sign of approval and support. The Lord showed me that just as they were flashing their headlights at me, so the cross was God's flashlight to them and to all who walk and live in darkness. He also showed me that the reason for the 40-day walk was to enable the cross to be etched in the people's minds, so that even when the walk was over, many would still see the cross as someone continues to see light or an image after they have stared at it for a while and then close their eyes or blink.

As I was turning into Lanark Way, four young Catholic boys shouted to me, 'Hey mister! Where are you going?' They went on to ask with some concern in their voices, 'Are you going down Lanark Way, mister?' I smiled at them and said, 'Yes, I've walked along the Falls Road, and now I'm going to walk along the Shankill Road.' One of the young men then said, 'They're all Orangees down there. They'll shoot you!' ('Orangee' is a slang name sometimes used for Protestants by some Catholics.) On hearing his concern for my safety I smiled at him and said, 'No, son, I'll be OK,' and then to their horror I walked into Lanark Way and through the security gate towards the Shankill community. I could imagine them thinking, 'That's the last we'll see of him, for he's walking straight into the green-eyed monster' – or should I say the orange-eyed monster!

As I began to walk along the Shankill Road, I was once again greeted by some of the local shoppers and motorists. One man in particular, who was standing at the front door of the Northern Ireland Social Club, shouted over to me, 'I'm proud of you.' Man, this made me feel so good. Not puffed up, but good. And while many others spoke similar words of encouragement, it is my belief that the uplifted cross was speaking louder to them than they were speaking to me.

Chapter Twelve

THE GOOD, THE BAD AND THE UGLY

In John 3:16 we are told, '. . . that whosoever believes in him [Jesus] should not perish, but have eternal life.' Day 35 was to confirm that the 'whosoever' were being touched by the witness of the cross being lifted in such a way. This was evidenced by the following encounters.

As I walked along the Falls Road two Catholic women and a young girl had been waiting for me. When I arrived where they had been standing one of the women said, 'God bless you, love. We're praying that God will give you the strength to finish.' They walked alongside me for about 50 yards and then turned down a street off the Falls Road. As they began to turn into the street they looked towards me and said, 'Goodbye and God bless.' I responded in kind.

Soon after this a car stopped alongside me with three nuns in it. The driver said, 'God bless you, Pastor, and a Happy Easter to you.' Again I responded in kind, wishing them a happy Easter before they drove off. As they did so I remembered a little maxim that is often repeated about magpies (black and white birds), but as Protestant kids growing up in Northern Ireland we used to say it about nuns (more black and white birds – sorry sisters)! It goes like this, 'One for sorrow, two for joy, three for a girl and four for a boy.' So having seen the three nuns I continued my walk along the Falls Road looking for a new girl, but nothing materialized! However, I still appreciated the greetings of the three sisters.

As I later walked along the Springfield Road I had one serious challenge from a man who made more of a fool of himself than the fool he was calling me! Three other men were with him, but they just stood and looked at him with embarrassment. While he was shouting and looking as if he was ready to burst a blood vessel, I purposely busied myself waving and speaking to other passers-by. I eventually turned to him and said, 'God loves you, brother,' but he continued to shout obscenities and to hurl what he obviously intended to be insults.

I then offered to step off the road and meet face to face with him on the pavement, not in a high-noon-style confrontation, but to speak sensibly with him. He responded with the same sense of rage and shouted, 'No, just stay where you are.' So I again told him that God loved him and then simply walked on, while those who were with him continued to display embarrassment, if not disgust.

A little further along the road another man stopped his car and stepped out in front of me with a camera, then took a picture as I walked past. He then wished me well and got back into his car. A police Land Rover then drove past, with the horn sounding a note of support for what I was doing. Shortly after this, two British Army Land Rovers drove by and as they did so I received an encouraging wave from both drivers. It was as if everyone was joining in!

Back on the Shankill Road there was much the same reception. When I got to the Rex Bar, a woman in her thirties stepped over the pavement and onto the road. I noticed an older woman standing in the street beside the bar. The younger woman met me on the road and placed money into my hand. She said, 'I know you are not collecting money, but that's my mother standing behind me. My father died recently, and my mother wanted to come and meet you. She wants to give you this money for the church.' I later learned that her father had committed his life to Christ just before he died.

In receiving the gift from this woman I made it clear that I was not collecting money and had not taken money from anyone during the Cross Walk. Although many offers had been made, they had all been graciously declined. Yet on this occasion I said I would make an exception and that the money would be placed directly into the church. I looked across to thank the mother and although she managed a smile there was just a look of sadness on her face. I thanked them and assured them of my prayers and those of New Life. I then said, 'God bless you both,' and continued walking the short distance that remained to the church.

However, before I arrived at New Life Fellowship, I noticed a white car driving towards me – I mean really driving towards me! As far as I could see there were four men in it. Those I could see clearly were rough-looking characters. In fact they were ugly, especially the driver. I could see the car coming towards me, but I held my ground and my nerve. I slowed my pace, but I continued to hold to the white line in the middle of the road.

As they got much closer to me the driver finally swerved the car away. He screwed his face at me and was mouthing expletives, while the others, including one young lad, just laughed. He had made the point that he at least was not happy with what I was doing on the Shankill Road, not so much with the cross, but by my very presence in the Shankill community.

I recognized him as one of the local commanders and 'trigger men' belonging to the UFF's C/Company that controlled the Lower Shankill at that time, although a major power shift was to occur during the next twelve months, as recorded in the closing chapters of this book. However, I prayed that he and his friends would be around during the next five days to see the cross still being uplifted daily without fear or wavering on my part, and that the sight of the cross would become etched on their minds.

This prayer was in fact answered, because a full year later a young lad who was in the car stopped me in the street and said, 'Hey Jackie! You remember when you carried the cross on the Shankill last year?' Then with a huge smile on his face he said, 'My da tried to knock you down!' His 'da' had fled to Scotland at that time, but not before he and his brother put bricks through the windows of my car and my son Jonathan's car for a reason I'll not go into. However, this was truly a situation where the cross in my hand was being lifted above the gun that is often in his hand.

Finally it was back to church for another incredible day of worship. In fact we had an amazing breakthrough in New Life that day as I preached on 'clearing the blockages' and 'breaking the hindrances'. The 'whosoever' had once again been out there on what was another fine day. Yet it seemed that on Day 35 it was just more noticeable, for on this day I met the good, the bad and the ugly. However, God loves them all and Christ died for them all.

This is the message of the cross and was the very reason why I did what I did, that all might know, no matter who they were and no matter what they had done with their lives, God loved them and Christ died for them. This continues to be the message of the cross.

•
An honour, but a struggle

The finish line was coming into focus with every passing day. I felt it was such an honour to have been chosen by God to raise the cross in such a manner as a public act of witness to His love and to the sacrifice of His Son. Yet the humanity in me was still struggling with fulfilling what I knew to be God's divine purpose and calling upon my life at that time. I understood what Paul meant when he said, 'For Christ's love compels us' (2 Cor 5:14).

Yet for some reason, as I once again walked through the security gate that would lead me to the Falls Road, I began again to feel a sense of apprehension, though I had no rational reason for this. I knew I had God's blessing and that His anointing was upon my life for this occasion, yet it seemed this was not sufficient to satisfy the natural need for human affirmation, and I was not disappointed.

Once again, on Day 36, there were those who welcomed me and greeted me from their cars and from the pavement. One motorist put his open hand right out of the window and held it there, waiting for me to return the compliment. Our hands slapped together at a combined speed of about 15 m.p.h.! Yet soon after this I again faced a negative reaction on the Springfield Road. This was from the same person and was at the same place as the previous day.

Again I could do no more than express the fact that God loved him. When he called me an idiot for carrying the cross, I immediately responded with, 'No, this is an honour. This is worth carrying and worth living for.' People on either side of the street smiled and waved their hands in that welcome affirmative manner. I continued with my walk to the sound of this man's enraged voice still filling the surrounding air. However, I prayed for him with the understanding that he was just like many others who were blinded by the god of this present age.

A little further along the Springfield Road there were three young men in their early to mid twenties who were watching me as they bit into their apples and sandwiches. I made the mistake of speaking to them (or perhaps it was no mistake). They reacted in much the same way as the previous person. They shouted obscenities and hurled insults at me. But again I blessed them in Jesus' name and then kept on walking until I got back through the security gate and back along the Shankill to the church.

The cobbler and Bone Yard

The following day was a glorious spring day! A glorious day for a walk, even if it was with a cross! Once again I was met with the now expected and familiar words of welcome and gestures of greeting. While three men were walking into a bar on the Falls Road one of them turned around and said, 'Y'all right, Jack?' This is a typical Northern Ireland greeting and was also typical of the day.

As I turned into the Springfield Road I was expecting the same verbal abuse of the previous two days, but thankfully it did not materialize. Instead, there were five young men in their late teens and early twenties who were keenly watching me walk towards them. One of these young men, in an act of good Irish banter, stepped to the edge of the pavement.

As I approached where he was standing he began to clap his hands and to cheer me on. 'Come on!' he shouted, 'We're all behind you. Keep it up now!' I smiled and spoke back to him. One of his friends then shouted out, 'Only three more days and then you're away from here!' I responded by saying, 'Yes, but the

cross won't. It will still be on your minds even after I've gone.'
They all smiled approvingly.

Soon after this encounter another group of young people
were passing by. One of them spoke up and said, 'Mister, how
long do you have to go now?' I answered, 'Just three more days
after this one.' A young woman shouted, 'Happy Days!' I said,
'No, Good Friday!' I am still not sure if she was happy for me that
I would soon complete the walk, or if she was just happy that I'd
soon be finished and would not be back!

Later, when I was walking back down the Shankill Road with
sweat dripping from me like gravy, there were once again plenty
of opportunities to greet people. The local cobbler was standing
at the front of his shop and was still hoping to get some business
out of me at the end of the walk. We bantered with each other
as I passed by with the cross. He asked how my shoes were
holding out. I responded, 'Better than I am!' He still managed a
smile though.

Then there was a guy by the name of Boneyard, who shouted
at me from his taxi as he drove up the Shankill Road and passed
me. Ten minutes later he stopped his car beside me as he drove
back down the road. This time he spoke out: 'Well, Jack, you're
nearly finished then.' I said, 'Yes, Boneyard – just a few more
days.' He said, 'Fair play to you, Jack. Keep it up now.' We
chatted briefly and then he drove on looking for his next fare. I
pray he will soon take Jesus on board!

As I finished the walk at the church and moved onto the pavement, I turned to speak with a man as he was walking past. His
wife Linda had been my secretary for a number of years and had
gone on a mission trip to Albania with Kathleen. Tragically Linda,
a mother of three boys, had died suddenly the previous year. I
spoke briefly with Stephen on the footpath. I could see it was

difficult for him to speak and that he was holding back the tears as he tried to share how he and his three boys were managing without Linda.

There are times when words are so empty and are just not enough. However, I pray that simply stopping with Stephen and chatting with him, albeit very briefly, was an encouragement to him and that the message of the cross would impact his life and the lives of so many other hurting people within the communities.

I pointed heavenward and walked on

As I began the walk the following day, Day 38, some friends from the USA – Colleen Mickey from San Diego, and Heather Collins and two other girls from Huntsville, Alabama – joined with me for the walk. They, like many others, had been emailing regularly and had been keeping up with all my reports, but now they were with me in person. It was a joy to have them along to pray in the church before the commencement of the walk and then to accompany me afterwards. The churches the girls had come from were among those that faithfully prayed for me as I pressed on with the walk daily.

Wednesdays are usually quiet, because many of the shops in Northern Ireland close all day or half the day. However, there was still enough traffic and people around to make an impact. As I began my walk along the Falls Road I was immediately welcomed by a passing motorist, who blasted his horn, put his hand out of the window and shouted, 'Well done, Pastor Jack.' Others were flashing their lights and waving. People on the pavement were responding positively as I greeted them.

Feeling quite confident, I turned to speak with another man who was walking along the pavement to my right. I looked him straight in the eye and said, 'Good morning, sir!' His sad-looking expressionless face immediately began to display a look of anger as he said, 'Don't talk to me ya f***ing Protestant b***!' Then he said, 'We'll not forget what ya's have f***ing done, ya b***!'

It then dawned on me that this was the same guy who'd had a go at me previously on the Springfield Road with the green, white and orange hat on his head. He did not have his hat on this day, so I failed to recognize him until he opened his mouth! I finally responded by saying to him, 'God loves you, brother.' I pointed heavenward and walked on as he continued to rant and rave! It seemed he still had a desire to rip off my head, and that part of his frustration was his inability to harm me. He was either under orders, or he was frightened of the two angels that some had claimed to have seen walk alongside me on the road.

I then continued along the Falls Road with the knowledge that God was using this to speak into the lives of many, even those who ranted and raved. A van with three workmen stopped alongside me. One of them asked me how many days I had left. Then a car with four people on board stopped and I think all four were shouting over the top of each other to wish me well. Another car stopped and the driver said, 'Fair play to you, mate.' Two police Land Rovers passed by and turned into a side street. They stopped and waited at the end of the street until I had walked past.

As I turned into Lanark Way a large truck stopped beside me. The driver, sitting high in his cab, opened his window and asked me what the walk was about. When I explained to him, he leaned right out of his window and stretched down to where I was standing and shook my hand. His firm grip said what he struggled to say with his mouth.

Soon I was walking through the gates at Lanark Way, along

with those who were now accompanying me. Although the Shankill Road, like the Falls Road, was much quieter than previous days, there were still enough people around to make it interesting and worthwhile. Most people were now aware of what I was doing, yet there were still those who were being inquisitive. However, I was thinking to myself, 'Two more days and the walk will be over, but the impact of the Cross Walk will continue.' While thinking it was almost over, God put a new challenge before me, which was every bit as challenging, if not more so, as doing the actual 40-day walk itself.

Into the Sinn Fein/IRA office

It was the following day, Day 39, that I went along to the Sinn Fein/IRA office on the Falls Road to present them with a gift. This was a major step on my part as this office was a representation of those who had been responsible for many deaths within the Shankill community, including some of my friends and at least two attempts on my own life as documented in my first book *Through Terror and Adversity*. Yet I felt it was important that I should not simply be seen to be walking past these offices carrying a cross 40 times over 40 days, but that I should also be willing to reach out to those who were the perceived enemies of the community that I was from.

The gift I brought was a mahogany framed mirror. On the glass was a Celtic cross along with the words from John 3:16 in the Irish language. As I stood pushing the buzzer and waiting for a response, the door was eventually opened to me. To my amazement and delight the man who stood in front of me was the same man who had come to our rescue when we had faced the serious confrontation on Day 29. He immediately recognized me and welcomed me with a hearty handshake.

After I explained why I was there he invited me in. He proceeded to show me around and to introduce me to some of those who were working within the offices. Everyone received me well as I was given this private and personalized, albeit unexpected, tour of the Sinn Fein offices. Before leaving, I expressed my appreciation to the people on the Falls Road for putting up with me during the 40 days of the Cross Walk.

I then asked if they would accept the mirror as a token of my appreciation. They were happy to receive it and expressed their delight that the Cross Walk had gone so well. I concluded by saying, 'Tomorrow I will finish the walk, but I hope this mirror will remain as a reminder of the message I have sought to bring during these 40 days.' We shook hands again, and then I went on my way.

Thirty minutes later I was walking back along the Falls Road and past the Sinn Fein offices, only this time I was in the middle of the road with the cross being held high for the penultimate day of the Cross Walk. I was immediately greeted by a driver who I *think* wanted to direct my attention Godward, although he used his middle finger to do so! 'Bless him!' I said to myself, as he insisted pointing heavenward using the middle finger of his right hand while driving with his left hand.

More and more people were speaking to me from their cars and from the pavement. Everyone seemed to know I was almost finished. Some were obviously delighted that I was successfully completing the 40 days, while others were simply glad I would soon be gone. However, it was just awesome as people wished me well for the last couple of days.

As I was walking along the Springfield Road I saw a group of seven young men. They were all in their late teens or early twenties, and were standing on the pavement looking in my direction. When I got up close to them, one of them walked to the edge of the pavement. I was ready for anything, as the young man was just standing there staring at me.

He eventually called out to me and said, 'Hey, does God really love everybody?' I immediately stopped and looked over to him. He again shouted, 'Does God really love everybody?' I then made my way across to where he was standing and said, 'Yes, God really does love everybody.' I went on to say, 'He loves me, but He loves you just as much as He loves me.' With his friends standing behind him, listening to every word, I went on to explain John 3:16.

When I told him that God so loved the world, he turned to his friends and shouted, 'See, I told you God loves everybody!' He then picked on one of them and said, 'See, Squeak, God does love everybody.' At this point I began to realize that he was under the influence of dope, but praise God he was still getting the message. He then turned to a man sitting in a car close by and shouted at him, 'Didn't I tell you? God loves everybody!' It seemed he had seen me walking with the cross on previous days and that this had moved him to tell his friends that God loves everyone. My response was the confirmation he was looking for and that he was in fact correct!

I then explained how we all need to believe and what it actually means to believe. I pointed out that it was not enough to believe with the head, but how it was necessary to believe with the heart. Then when it was time for me to move on, I asked him his name. He said, 'My name is Mickey.' I said, 'Mickey! I'm going to be praying for you and for Squeak and for the rest of your friends.' He thanked me. We shook hands and I went back to the centre of the road with the cross. As I began walking along the road again I could still hear him saying to his friends, 'You see, I was right. God does love everybody.' I smiled and prayed for him and for his friends as I proceeded with the walk.

Soon after this I was called aside by a man sitting in his car. He had been waiting to speak with me. He introduced himself as Cairan from Andersonstown. He told me he had been living in San Jose, California, for several years, but that he was back home on holiday. He said, 'I couldn't believe my eyes when I saw you walking along the road carrying the cross.' He then asked, 'Why are you doing this?' After I gave him my well-trodden explanation, he reached out his hand and taking hold of mine he said, 'Good on you, mate!' We then talked for a while and said we would keep in touch with each other, which we have.

Soon it was back to the Shankill, where things were much the same. On the Shankill Road it was usually not much more than a passing greeting, whereas on the Falls and Springfield Roads it was more likely to lead to a conversation. However, the witness was still strong as the cross was faithfully lifted above the wall of division that towered between the communities and also above the gun that was the instrument of that division.

The final day of the Cross Walk

Well, the final day of the Cross Walk had arrived at last. At one time it had felt as though this day would never come. However, now that it was finally here it did not really feel as if it had been six weeks since the Cross Walk began. Yet at the same time, it also felt as if I had been doing this for ever. This had been such an amazing experience for me personally, and had touched the lives of more people than I will ever know this side of eternity.

On Day 39 I had taken the mirror containing the cross and

John 3:16 into the Sinn Fein office on the Falls Road, but on Day 40 the Shankill awakened to a 25-foot wooden cross standing tall at the bottom of the Shankill Road. We had finally completed erecting this large cross at midnight, and right next to the New Life Fellowship church. It stands alongside our New Life mural and together they are the first things that people see as they enter the Shankill Road from downtown Belfast. It looks so stunning and continues to grab the attention of many passers-by. It has also become pictorially interesting to tourists and presents a welcome alternative to the murals depicting the gun.

So although the 40-Day Cross Walk has come to an end, the cross is still being uplifted in some way, both within the Falls community in the Sinn Fein office (hopefully the mirror is hanging on one of their walls) and also within the Shankill community, where a 25-foot cross is most definitely hanging on a wall and it stands as a silent and powerful witness to the love of God and to the sacrifice of Jesus Christ, His Son.

As I commenced the last day of the walk I wondered how people would react. It soon became quite apparent that many were aware that this was the last day. Many reminded me of this fact as they passed by in cars or on the pavement. Many would say, 'Well done, Pastor,' or, 'Well done, Jack.' I had more hand-shakes and hand smacks on this day than on any other day during the walk. Cairan, whom I met the previous day, met with me again today. He accompanied me in his car along the entire route from the Falls Road to the bottom of the Shankill Road. Several times he stopped his car and got out to film my walk with the cross.

It turned out that Cairan is a professor in the USA and has a digital imaging/multimedia business in San Jose. His name is Cairan MacGowan and he is also a singer/songwriter. In fact he gave me some of his CDs, one with a song of peace for Northern Ireland on it.

Anyway, this was perhaps the easiest day of the walk. The weather was kind to me, the people on both sides of the wall were friendly, and even the truck drivers were well behaved. Then to top it all, as I was approaching the bottom end of the Shankill Road, I could see people standing at the corner of New Life church. The closer I got, the more I could see that a crowd of people had been waiting for me. Pastor Eric McComb, my superintendent, was there. Then there were a number of other pastors and their wives, along with members from other churches and some from New Life Fellowship. They gave me such a welcome as I finished those final steps that it helped me appreciate again just how much people had been supportive during those days. This was totally unexpected on my part, but was nonetheless very much appreciated.

I therefore want to place on record my sincere thanks to all who were there for me, not just at the end of the walk, but throughout the 40 days; to those who prayed for me, who sent emails or made phone calls, and to those who spoke with me on the road. This was as much a journey for those who stood with me in prayer and for those who walked with me in spirit as it had been for me.

My prayer is that we will all respond to the ongoing challenge to take up the cross and follow Christ. Not so much one made of wood, but one that is evidenced in our lifestyle and our daily walk before God and before men. And that we will continue to lift the message of love above the message of hatred; that we will continue to lift the message of reconciliation above the message of division, and that we will continue to lift the message of the cross above the message of the gun.

However, having made this challenge, I must admit that sadly and tragically for some, the sound of the gun would once again be heard in Belfast and with fatal consequences for the Shankill and for other communities. It therefore saddens me that I have to conclude with the following two chapters, but the reality is that the gun is not silenced in Belfast. Peace has been much talked about; a 'man-made' Good Friday 'Agreement' has been entered into; documents have been signed. Yet it seems to have been done without the 'binding' components, for the gun is not silenced.

Yet for all that, in the words of a Chris Bowater song, 'The cross still stands. The cross still towers. His blood still cleanses; eternally the same.'

Chapter Thirteen

BROTHER AGAINST BROTHER

The book of Genesis, the first book of the Bible, gives design and purpose to the existence of the universe and to life itself. It also provides an explanation for the emergence of evil and how it universally and thoroughly affected all of creation, including the introduction of human conflict. The first murder in human history is recorded in the fourth chapter of the book of Genesis. This was not the result of conflict between enemies, but of conflict between brothers, Cain and Abel, the sons of Adam and Eve.

It has often been said that blood is thicker than water, suggesting that the closer the relationship the greater the bond. However, the story of Cain and Abel shows that a strong blood relationship can break under the wrong kind of pressure. This was further evidenced in the strained relationship that existed between Jacob and his older twin brother Esau, and although with God's help they finally managed to resolve their differences, the fact is that their descendants did not.

The Israelites and the Edomites were descendants of Isaac the son Abraham, but the Israelites were descended through Jacob the son of Isaac, whereas the Edomites were descended through Jacob's twin brother Esau, thus making the Israelites and the Edomites cousins, if you like. Yet in spite of their obvious blood relationship they became historical enemies. These became two separate nations descended from one set of twins. They should have been looking out for each other, as relatives normally do, but several times throughout their troubled history they feuded and fought against each other.

The same could be said of modern-day Israelis and most Arab nations, who are brothers in the sense that they are descended from Abraham. The Israelis are descended from Abraham and Sarah through Isaac and Jacob, whereas many of the Arab nations are descended from Abraham, including those born to Hagar through the line of Ishmael and his twelve sons. Yet though they all claim Abraham as their father, they have been warring against each from the day and hour they came into existence. History therefore reveals that relationships can often sadly and tragically breakdown, even to the point of brother turning against brother.

Northern Ireland has always been known for its conflict between Catholics and Protestants, but more for political reasons. However, there have been many times throughout the period referred to as 'The Troubles' when Catholic has turned against Catholic and Protestant has turned against Protestant. This has often been due to the falling out of paramilitary organizations within the respective Republican and Loyalist communities. These 'fall outs' have been referred to as feuds due to the nature of their internal conflict.

A further demise in Loyalism

However, it seemed the lessons from the Loyalist feud in 2000 had not been properly understood, for in two short years, by September 2002, there was another upsurge of feudal violence within Loyalism. Once again this was to lead to further death and destruction at the hands of fellow Loyalists, as brother turned against brother. This in turn led to a further demise in Loyalism and Unionism within Northern Ireland. At one time their emblazoned common cry was 'United we stand, divided we fall', and if this comment is correct then the entire structure that embraces Loyalism, Unionism and historical Protestantism is collapsing within Northern Ireland.

One of the first persons to die in the early days of this new feud was a father of six children and a one-time friend of Gordie, a leader within New Life Fellowship, who at the time of his friend's murder was with our worship team in the USA. His car had been hit 15 times. His three-year-old daughter was in the back seat at the time of the shooting, but thankfully the little girl was not injured physically.

While we were still in the USA we received news of another man who had been shot in the face in a separate incident, but he mercifully survived the murder bid. This man was, and still is, quite well known within paramilitary 'Loyalism'. It soon came to light that this was part of the emerging Loyalist feud and was connected to an attempt by one person to secure the supreme command of the UFF within Belfast.

As the Protestant communities being affected by this fresh upsurge of violence were trying to come to terms with this new feud, the IRA took advantage of the situation and attempted to murder another Protestant, but he also survived the attack on his life. Immediately following this, three Catholics were shot and wounded by Loyalist paramilitaries in retaliation for this attack. However, in spite of these shootings the main focus at that time was not Protestant against Catholic or the reverse, but Loyalist against Loyalist, and more specifically UFF against UFF.

Welcome news

On the Sunday night after our return from the USA, a young woman attended New Life Fellowship for the first time. This young woman has several brothers who are all members of the UFF within the Lower Shankill community, an area that was central to the developing feud in more ways than one. Speaking with me after the service she said, 'Jack, you don't know how much you impacted the paramilitaries on the Shankill Road when you carried that cross.'

She went on to explain how she heard several positive comments from paramilitary members about the Cross Walk. It was such an encouragement to know that after a period of six months the Cross Walk was still being talked about and was still impacting lives within the Shankill community. While the gun was once again being fired in anger within the Shankill community, the cross was still being remembered.

Tensions worsen

On 29th September 2002 the UFF leadership in Northern Ireland expelled one of their senior brigadiers, who was also one of the leading terrorists within Northern Ireland, from the organization. He was commander of the infamous and often-times ruthless C/Company, based within the Lower Shankill community. Once again trouble had come to roost on our doorstep. The other brigadiers publicly denounced the C/Company commander as the main rival behind the emerging feud. This led to further public and oftentimes angry accusations and counter-accusations being openly expressed, as those involved within the leadership of the organization were willing to point the finger of blame at those they deemed responsible. There was no doubt that this would eventually lead to a situation where the brigadier of C/Company, Johnny Adair, would be deposed and removed.

Many wondered, as I had done at that time, what this would mean for the Lower Shankill community where Adair and many of his close associates lived, and where his headquarters was based. This is also where our church and youth centre are situated and where several of our members live, including my own mother, two brothers and their families, Kathleen's sister and her husband.

However, to add to our concerns, we also had a team of 14 Americans visiting us from the Second Mile Centre in Philadelphia. We were concerned about their safety, as they were staying within the Lower Shankill community close to our church. Tensions were running very high throughout the Shankill, and we were uncertain as to how events would unfold. Thankfully, while the pot was boiling, the lid remained firmly in place until our friends had left for home. But soon the lid would come off, and more deaths would be recorded.

Political mayhem

While the Loyalist feud was worsening, so too was the political situation, although the two were not directly connected. Politics

in Northern Ireland were at an all-time low and the political insti-
tutions were about to collapse. The people of Northern Ireland
had been given a promise of a better and more secure future.
They were promised an end to the conflict, with peace as the
ultimate prize, but they were now helplessly looking on as the
'peace process', now almost five years on, was beginning to
collapse.

Terrorist organizations on all sides were failing to make the
transition from violence to non-violence and from their favourite
choice of weapon to the ballot box of democracy. While present-
ing a semblance of turning they were becoming more
entrenched in organized crime, including major drug-running
operations and the control of communities within Belfast and
across Northern Ireland. Of course the godfathers and the
spokespersons for these organizations will each deny this, but so
too did Al Capone and Vito and Michael Corleone!

These same organizations would also seek to use more
reputable methods to provide themselves with a cloak of respectability, such as running legitimate businesses or community
organizations, where some of their members were and are
employed as youth and community workers. But who wants to
know?

While the feud within Loyalism was worsening, the IRA
continued to pose a major threat to any chance of lasting and
permanent peace within Northern Ireland. During the peace
process the IRA continued to secure weapons in Florida, where
some of their colleagues had been arrested and finally imprisoned for gun-running. During the same time frame three of their
members/colleagues were arrested in Columbia for allegedly
training FARC terrorists in bomb making. However, after several
years on remand they were finally acquitted of terrorist offences,

but were found guilty of entering Columbia on false passports. Yet again during the same time frame the Special Branch offices in Belfast were broken into and highly confidential information was stolen. All fingers were and still are pointing to the IRA.

Then to top it all, once again during the same time frame referred to as 'the peace process', members of Sinn Fein/IRA were arrested in various parts of Belfast. The Sinn Fein office based in Stormont (Northern Ireland's Assembly (Government) Building) was raided by police officers. It has subsequently been alleged that certain members of staff had been involved in intelligence gathering that had gone to the highest levels of government within the United Kingdom, and particularly Northern Ireland. Responding to this, David Trimble, the leader of the largest Unionist Party (at that time) and a supporter of the peace process said, 'This is more serious than Watergate.'

Further development

Due to the above set of circumstances it became evident that on Monday 14th October 2002 it would be announced that the Northern Ireland Assembly would be suspended. This would mean that political responsibility would return to the British parliament in Westminster, England. While many of us would be content with this we nonetheless recognized that politically this would have its drawbacks. However, we did not quite know what this would mean for the peace process. Concerns were raised that the political fall-out would create a vacuum and would present an opportunity for the terrorists to return to violence. Yet if they were committed to peace, as they had been claiming, then the peace process would continue in spite of the political stalemate.

It was at that time that some of us within New Life Fellowship felt challenged to take our prayers to the seat of political power in Northern Ireland. So on Monday 14th October 2002, a number of us gathered on the steps of Stormont to pray and to call upon the various politicians who were gathering, perhaps for the last time in this format, to 'get it right' for the sake of the people in Northern Ireland. Holding large billboards containing the names of all the political parties and the names of their respective leaders and with the words 'We are praying for you', we held our prayer vigil at the front of Stormont from 9 a.m. until 12 noon.

Our presence did not go unnoticed, as we thought it might. In fact we were approached by quite a number of television crews and photojournalists, etc. Many of those going into the building for this historical meeting had to pass us before going through the front entrance. Some walked past us as if we were the idiots, although I have to concede that they were the ones getting paid for being there, and handsomely at that! Others managed a cursory glance with a sheepish and reluctant salutation.

However, others did take the time to approach us and speak with us at length. These included certain members of Sinn Fein/IRA, who thanked us for being there and for praying for them! We told them we were happy to pray for them, but reminded them of their responsibility to make correct decisions for the future of Northern Ireland.

Then there was Cedric Wilson, leader of the Northern Ireland Unionist Party, who encouraged us to keep on praying. Nigel Dodds of the Democratic Unionist Party, and Member of Parliament (MP) for North Belfast, also stopped with us for a chat. He likewise encouraged us to keep up the good work and to keep on praying. The only woman to stop and speak with us was Eileen Bell of the Northern Ireland Alliance Party. She told us she also had been praying for the situation and thanked us for doing so. She went on to say, 'You know, I thought that given the seriousness of the situation many more people would have been here today, but only you have turned up to pray.'

So our efforts were not in vain, for in the midst of all the political mayhem we managed to get our message across, be it on television or personally and directly to some of the politicians, but only they could determine the outcome of their meeting.

Before the end of the day, the Northern Ireland Assembly was suspended and Northern Ireland was once again beginning another undetermined period of Direct Rule from the British parliament at Westminster. This would eventually lead to fresh elections that would see the demise of the Ulster Unionist Party (UUP) as more Unionists would favour the Democratic Unionist Party (DUP), and also the demise of the Social Democratic Labour Party (SDLP) as more Catholics would favour Sinn Fein. Only time will tell if there will be another change in the fortunes of these political parties, and if things will really improve for the people in Northern Ireland. In the meantime, the feud within the UFF was still hotting up.

Cops for Christ

While the above feud and the political mayhem was still going on and seemingly worsening with each passing day, we continued to receive visitors from the USA to work alongside us at New Life Fellowship and within the Shankill community. Among these were four Floridians and three New Yorkers. It had been intended for them to stay in two of our apartments close to the church, but due to the unrest relating to the UFF feud we felt it would be more appropriate to accommodate them in our home and in the home of our daughter Chara (Cara) and her husband Les. The team was led by Mike DiSanza (President of Cops for Christ) and Bobby McIntosh (Smithtown Gospel Tabernacle, Long Island NY).

Immediately following their safe departure we had a visit from Tim and Meg Britton of the New Life Church in Colorado Springs. They are both involved in ministry at the New Life Church, with Meg being the personal secretary to Pastor Ted Haggard. Tim's mother, Virginia, was also with them. We had a wonderful time with them in spite of the unrest within the community. Also, and without going into detail, their visit was very timely for Kathleen and me, and was much appreciated.

At the very same time we had a visit from Pastor Gerry Shannon and his wife Silvia of the New Harvest Church in Surry, Virginia. We praise God that in spite of all the shenanigans going on around us we still managed to have a blast (excuse the pun) as all our visitors ministered right into the heart and the hurts of our church.

Young man crucified

Pastor Gerry Shannon accompanied me one night on a visit to the Royal Victoria Hospital in Belfast. We went to visit three young men. The first was Darren. He was only 17 and was fighting for his life after a serious car accident. His girlfriend had been attending New Life Fellowship, where she had committed her life to Christ some three months earlier. She had finally got Darren to agree to come along to church with her on a Sunday night, but it was two days before on Friday morning that Darren was in a serious car accident.

While the doctors were doing all they could to save him they would give no indication of hope. Yet against all the odds Darren managed to pull through. He did so with the help of the doctors and nurses who cared for him, and also with the prayers of his parents, his girlfriend and many Christians who believed in the power of prayer. Today he is doing well and is now attending New Life Fellowship where, like Paula, he has committed his life to Christ. They are now engaged to be married.

The second young man we went to visit was Lee, who was Darren's friend. Lee had two broken legs and four broken ribs, as well as sustaining head injuries, although, unlike Darren, Lee was not fighting for his life. Lee was also discharged from hospital, and although I have not seen him since, as he lives elsewhere in Northern Ireland, I understand he is doing well.

The third young man was Harry. Wow! Listen to this one! Harry was a young Catholic lad who had been crucified. That's right, crucified! It had initially been thought the IRA had carried out this barbaric act, first because Harry was apparently a well-known joy-rider within west Belfast, an area controlled by the IRA. It was therefore thought he was a victim of an IRA punishment squad. Secondly, it was believed the IRA were responsible because they had previously crucified a young Catholic man in north Belfast.

However, it soon came to light that Harry had in fact been beaten and finally crucified by a group of seven so-called Protestants. They had apparently caught him in the act of steal-ing a car in their area. They beat him and then nailed him to a wooden post with six-inch nails, bending them inwards so he could not get away. They broke both his legs and beat him so badly that he was almost dead when help finally arrived.

He and his family were delighted that Pastor Gerry and I had called to visit him, particularly that a Protestant minister from the Shankill Road would do so. We were thankful for the opportunity to speak with this young man and his family and to pray with them before leaving.

God's grace in the midst of violence

December 12th, 2002 and Christmas was looming, but still the feuding and the violence continued. This included the 'regular' punishment beatings and shootings by the terrorists within their respective communities. It also included the tragic shooting dead of a man in Ballygowan after his six-year old son unwittingly opened the front door of his home to the two gunmen who would murder his father.

The Lower Shankill UFF brigadier was still under a lot of pressure and was not making things any easier as he sought to weed out those around him he thought he could no longer trust. His attention even turned to some of his very close associates, particularly his second in command, who was forced to leave the lower Shankill community along with his entire family circle.

Bomb scare at mum's

I had parked my car alongside another that had been parked right next to my mother's home. I stayed with her for two hours before returning home. In the early hours of the following morning my mother was awakened by police officers, who explained to her that the car at the front of her home was a suspected car bomb. She immediately made her way to my brother's home nearby.

For almost four hours the army bomb disposal team worked at the suspected car bomb. They fired several shots into the car and placed three separate detonators on it in the hope that if there was a bomb it would go off. However, having established that the car did not contain a bomb, the army finally declared the area safe, and my mother was able to return home. This was nothing new to her, although she was no doubt shaken by the experience, but we were thankful it ended as it did.

We later discovered that the owner of the car had in fact been arrested after he had fired several shots into a bar in downtown Belfast. He had actually parked the car outside my mother's home with the intention of going off to shoot someone and then return again for the car. The shooting incident was linked to the ongoing UFF feud.

Neighbour's home attacked

It was a cold December Sunday evening. Our home was packed as usual after the Sunday evening service. We had finished with tea and refreshments and were settling down to play Balderdash when the calm night air was shattered with the sound of gunfire. We knew it was close, but only when we ran into the street did we know how close. The neighbour living two doors above us had only just taken his children to bed. As soon as he walked back into his living room, several shots were fired through his window, narrowly missing him and his wife.

Soon after this and two days before Christmas 2002, a 35-year-old father was shot in the neck. He was one of our past participants of an eight-week Higher Force Challenge programme. His children had also attended our pre-school Hobby Horse Playgroup. Thankfully his wounds were not fatal, but his shooting nonetheless provided a further reminder that the UFF feud was far from over and that it might well lead to death for some unfortunate person or persons within our community.

Predictions are correct

Sadly, as I had been predicting while publicly expressing my concerns about the ongoing UFF feud, the fall-out did in fact lead to another death just two days after Christmas. The victim was a young man by the name of Jonathan Stewart. He was only 22 years of age. To my knowledge and from what others had been saying about his murder, Jonathan Stewart was not a member of any of the terrorist organizations. It seemed the shooting had been carried out by some of those connected to the Lower Shankill C/Company of the UFF. One name in particular has been mentioned, but no one has been charged.

A couple of nights later, while working at my computer, a military helicopter was flying overhead, low enough to make our home tremor. On hearing this I realized that something else must have happened, and sure enough two streets away shots had been fired into another home. This time it was another member of C/Company who had in fact been shot. He was wounded in the hand and his wife had been shot in the back, but their injuries were not life threatening and they both survived the attack. It was alleged that this shooting was carried out in retaliation for the murder of Jonathan Stewart.

A call to prayer

When Sunday came around again I felt it was not enough simply to conduct church services in the midst of the violence, injuries and deaths, but that we as a church needed to respond more openly to the situation. I therefore called the church to prayer immediately following our Sunday evening service. This was not just to say prayers, but to seek the face of God on behalf of the

Shankill community and for direction as to what we should do in helping to bring the feud to an end.

During the main evening service a senior commander belonging to C/Company was in attendance. He said afterwards, 'All the questions I had ever asked about God were answered by Pastor Jack during his sermon.' He further said that he kept his eyes open during the appeal for salvation, as he was afraid he might raise his hand! His wife, who was with him, also remarked that she had never experienced the presence of God before, but she did that night.

During the prayer time afterwards we had an amazing encounter with God. As we sang and worshipped together, one by one people came to the microphone to pray for the Shankill community. Some wrote on pieces of paper what they believed God was saying to them and to the church. In the midst of the prayer and worship the Lord gave us clear direction concerning what our response should be to the ongoing situation.

The following day we began to put some of these things into action. The first thing I did was to visit Johnny Adair and speak with him and four of his men. He received me quite well, while instructing one of his men to make me a coffee. I talked with him about the ongoing situation and how tragic it was that lives were again being lost. He was in agreement with everything I was saying, and even expressed his sadness that lives were being lost and that Loyalist was fighting Loyalist, but he was also quite sure as to where the responsibility lay for the feud and clearly pointed the finger of blame at others. Unfortunately, there was no regret or acceptance of responsibility on his part for recent deaths and shootings.

I then took the opportunity to share with him and his associates what I believed God's perspective was on all of this. I also let them know that New Life Fellowship was praying for them and the entire situation. They seemed somewhat stunned and even speechless as I talked to them about God. They were much more comfortable talking about politics or the feud than about God. Nonetheless I had their ear. I believe God also had their attention in those moments and that in the midst of the violence men of the gun were listening to a man of the cross, albeit out of courtesy.

Later that day and unconnected to my earlier visit, two young women from our church also called to speak with Johnny Adair. They approached his home with some apprehension, not knowing what to expect. They took him a video cassette that contained the testimony of a Mafia boss in America who had committed his life to Christ, but they were not sure if Johnny would accept it. However, their concerns were soon allayed, as he came to the door and greeted them with a smile.

After they introduced themselves they handed him the tape and told him that New Life Fellowship was praying for him and his family. He received the gift with a smile and thanked them. As the girls left, they walked off holding hands and weeping nervously due to the emotion of the moment, but they had done a good thing – no, they had done a *God* thing! This was their way of lifting the message of the cross above the message of the gun. Johnny Adair was unable to see our light shine as we gathered inside the church building, but he sure saw it shine the day we went in obedience to where he was.

However, tensions continued to run high as one tragic incident was followed by another. The funeral of Jonathan Stewart, murdered by members of Adair's C/Company, was soon to be followed by the funeral of Roy Green, who was shot in the back of the head in retaliation for the above murder. Yet Roy Green was not even remotely involved in the murder of Jonathan Stewart. During this time I, as did others, appeared on television calling for an end to the feud. However, the wounds were so deep that no one within the UFF was ready or even willing to listen to any plea for calm.

Special prayer

The violence continued into the New Year. We held a special late night prayer service on the first Friday of 2003. We took a leaf from the Colorado Spring's World Prayer Centre's website by putting together a PowerPoint presentation of prayer requests that helped to unify our praying and keep us focused. As well as praying for local needs, but more specifically for an end to the ongoing violence and an end to the UFF feud, we also prayed for situations in other parts of the world.

We prayed for requests from the USA, particularly focusing on the families of three American missionaries who were murdered in Yemen and for a husband and his wife whose 29-year-old son Martin was shot dead in front of his wife and children, along with three others, by Muslim terrorists in Somalia. So while we were contending with the effects of the UFF feud within the Shankill and other communities, violence for religious reasons was sadly still ongoing in other parts of the world.

We also prayed for the advancing conflict in Iraq, knowing it would lead to the certain death of many. We prayed that war would be averted, yet we also accepted the inevitability of war as a consequence of man's inhumanity to man and as a constant unfolding of nation rising against nation and kingdom rising against kingdom as indicators of the end of the age and as predicted by Jesus Christ.

Johnny Adair's home attacked

At the end of the first week of January 2003 the home of Johnny Adair was attacked. A pipe bomb was thrown, exploding at the back of Adair's house, but it caused little damage and no injuries. However, the point was well made that those who wanted him dead were getting closer. Soon after this, one of his associates was shot several times and was critically wounded, but he survived the attack.

Three days later, on 10th January, Johnny Adair was arrested. He had previously been released from prison on licence as part of the peace process, but was finally re-arrested for allegedly directing acts of terror, i.e. the UFF feud. His licence was revoked and he was again imprisoned until January 2005.

Praying in the den of lions

While sensing the increased tension within the community, my assistant pastor, Mark Armstrong, and I discussed what we should do as a church in order to help bring the situation to an end. We looked again at suggestions made by our people at the special prayer time mentioned above. We decided we should call the church to a four-week prayer walk that would take us right into the lion's den.

The following day, Saturday 1st February, we were to learn that the arrest and imprisonment of Johnny Adair had not brought an end to the violence and deaths. In fact the situation was to worsen. Whether orders were being relayed from prison, or whether the person who took over as military commander of the Lower Shankill was now calling the shots, one of Johnny's main opponents, the UDA/UFF brigadier of South East Antrim, was gunned down and fatally wounded. Three other men who were with him in the car were also shot. For one of them, his wounds likewise proved fatal.

My concern was that these deaths might take our community over the brink and would probably bring horrifying repercussions upon the Lower Shankill community. I spoke again with Pastor Mark, as these latest murders seemed to add a new depth to the UFF feud and put a whole new perspective on anything we might decide to do as a church. I wondered if we should go ahead with inviting people to prayer walk the streets at night, as this would now be much more dangerous.

Mark said to me, 'I understand how you feel, but if it was God's will last night that we should put this to the church on Sunday morning then in spite of what has happened tonight it is still His will that we should do so.' Of course he was correct. I just needed some reassurance that it was not just me trying to lead people into something that was not of God.

So on Sunday morning I put it to the church. The response was just what we had expected. Almost 50 people volunteered to join with us as we prayer walked the streets of the Lower Shankill community for the next four weeks between the hours of 9.00 p.m. and 12 midnight. In addition to this, and in light of recent deaths and the worsening situation, I issued the following press release the next morning:

PRESS RELEASE
Monday 3 February 2003

In light of the recent UDA feud that has already claimed the lives of four people, Shankill pastor Jack McKee has called on his people, in the New Life Fellowship church, to become more active within the Lower Shankill community.

Today, every home will receive an open letter, addressed to the residents of the Lower Shankill, which will outline the intentions of members of New Life Fellowship church to walk the streets in teams of three and four each night between 9.00 p.m. and 12 midnight. Each team member will be wearing a white armband with a red cross. They will be praying for the community as they walk through the streets and will offer themselves to help in whatever way necessary.

Pastor Jack is also calling on other church leaders throughout the city of Belfast to do likewise within their respective areas, and to so mobilize their people that hundreds will be prayerfully walking the streets each night.

Pastor Jack is also calling upon all who are involved in the feud to think seriously about where they are taking their families and the communities at large, and to step back from the brink before more life is lost. An eye for an eye will leave us all blind, and a life for a life will eventually leave us all dead.

Chapter Fourteen

LIGHT AMID THE DARK

Monday 3rd February arrived and the first thing we did was visit every home throughout the Lower Shankill community and leave a copy of the open letter, mentioned above, which outlined our intentions for the following four weeks. I also made sure that anyone else who needed to know of our plans had likewise been informed. This included the media (radio and TV interviews), the police, the British army, the residents, the UFF in the Lower Shankill and their rivals with whom they had been feuding. In fact I actually went to a bar in north Belfast to see some of the commanders in that area and give them a copy of the open letter so that they would also know that we were on the streets within the Lower Shankill. This was not for their benefit, but for ours!

That same night we began our prayer walk, and what a start! We had barely taken three steps before a woman called out to us from her home. Her daughter had been badly beaten by her husband and was in intensive care. She told her daughter that the church had put letters into the homes and that she would call us to pray for her. This we did and later requested that others would do so.

Within a few minutes we were walking through what had become known as 'Johnny Adair's street'. The tension was incredible. A number of men approached us in the darkened street, but on recognizing us (the armbands with the cross were a big clue) they grudgingly grunted out the word, 'hi'. We returned the greeting, only without the grunt, and walked on. Within moments there were more men, but it was the same routine as before. They knew who we were and why we were there.

I then noticed their local community office was open, so I decided to go in and speak with whoever might be there. Unchallenged, I walked through the door and into the front room. To my surprise I saw three men standing with their back to the door! They were talking away to each other and were oblivious to the fact that I had walked in off the street. They only became aware of my presence when I spoke to them. On recognizing one of them I quickly spoke out and said, 'Hi, John!' John White, who was to Johnny Adair what Butch Cassidy was to the Sundance Kid (no insult meant to either twosome), immediately turned around and greeted me quite warmly. We stood and chatted for a while.

John and Johnny were more like The Odd Couple or some would say Bonnie and Clyde. You seldom saw one without the other. John was Johnny's number one spokesperson and comrade. He and Johnny had both been told to leave the country or die. They had received several threats on their lives that were relayed to them by the police. John thanked me for putting the letters into the homes within the area, and then told me how brave he thought we were and wished us well!

There were six of us (two teams of three) on that first night of the prayer walk. This is how it would be for most of the subsequent nights during the following four weeks. We walked through the snow, sometimes blizzard-like, and prayed from 9.00 p.m. through to midnight. Two other women who attend another church, but who live within the Lower Shankill, put their coats on and joined us on the walk. They also wore our specially made white armbands with a cross down the centre of them. The armbands helped to identify us to all within the community including the security forces, the paramilitaries and the residents. But they also gave us a sense of purpose, which was that of lifting the cross above the gun.

A feeling of despair

I never thought I would say it, but the following night I felt a real sense of despair. The situation seemed to be worsening with each passing hour. Many of the decent people, and there are many, within the Lower Shankill were living in fear of their lives.

An ultimatum had been issued by the leadership of the UDA, giving all of the men in Johnny Adair's C/Company 48 hours to stand up against him and his close associates or to face the consequences. This presented the rank and file membership of C/Company not only with a challenge, but also with a major dilemma. There was no doubt that to rise up against the leadership would put their lives at risk, but not to do so would equally put their lives in danger, and of course the lives of their families. Many of them felt trapped.

For many it would mean having to leave their homes and jobs and transfer to another company within the UDA/UFF. Most of these men were only nominal members, but they were trapped and did not know which way to turn. Even those who were not involved in the feud or not connected to the paramilitaries were in danger of becoming targets. This included some of our church and family members who lived within the area.

That night, amid the growing tension and the increased fear, I had managed to arrange a meeting with two senior members of the UDA/UFF in another part of the Shankill community. At first they had refused to meet with me saying they did not want to be told by me what they should or should not do. After assurances that this would not be my approach they agreed to meet with me. My approach was to make a simple appeal on behalf of those whose voices were silent through fear. My plea was that whatever the UDA were planning to do against the Lower Shankill, they would bear in mind the fact that most people living within the Lower Shankill were innocent and were living in fear, including most of Johnny Adair's rank and file C/Company members.

While they received me cautiously but warmly, their response was anything but encouraging. They made it clear that recent deaths would be avenged, particularly that of the South East Antrim brigadier, whose funeral would take place two days later and would be attended by some 10 to 20,000 men. It was also being suggested quite clearly that after the funeral on Thursday afternoon, the 10 to 20,000 UDA members who were expected to be in attendance would invade the Lower Shankill community. The meeting only served to confirm my worst fears.

I focused again on my appeal for the innocent to be spared. After giving me 50 minutes of their time, the meeting ended. Immediately following this I made my way to some of the homes within the Lower Shankill to try to encourage some of those living there. I then met up with our two prayer walk teams and spent the next three hours walking the streets with them and praying over a community that had seen more than its share of violence and death, but with the knowledge that it might well see more in the not-too-distant future.

The following day, however, I received a phone call from someone representing the two men I had met with on the previous evening. I was told that while I was meeting with them, two cars were preparing to enter the Lower Shankill community carrying armed men who were to shoot and kill the first two men they saw and then get out pronto. However, immediately after their meeting with me they contacted the men in the cars and called off the attack. It was made clear to me that two lives were spared that night. So if for no other reason this made the four-week prayer walk worth every step and every prayer. Yet, even more amazing developments were at hand.

A sudden end to the feud

That same day, Wednesday 5th February, was a day of interviews, phone calls and meetings with other senior UDA personnel. Most of it was very positive. However, from what I had been hearing during the day and in the early evening, I became concerned that an attempt might be made on the life of a prominent person within the Lower Shankill. My guess was John White, and I think that the way he had surrounded himself with C/Company pawns, he was also thinking along the same lines. Tensions were again running high by the time I met up with the prayer walk teams at 9.00 p.m.

The UDA ultimatum given to its C/Company members living within the Lower Shankill was having an impact in terms of fear among those who were opposed to the feud and felt trapped for one reason or another. Several men did in fact make the move. They jumped ship by leaving the Lower Shankill community and joining themselves to the other UDA companies that were based in mid and upper Shankill. Homes had been vacated and much talk was circulating naming those who had left. Throughout the night, many others were to jump ship. This served to increase the fear of those who remained behind and were still uncertain as to what they should do.

During our prayer walk I stopped with some of the C/Company members who were still on duty in 'Johnny's street' and encouraged them to take care during the night. While talking with two of them I said to the one I knew, 'Listen, Sammy; if anyone comes into this street tonight, for goodness' sake get off side. You're not going to stop anyone who comes at you with guns.' The person alongside him immediately slapped his side, and revealing a gun in his belt, he said, 'Let the b*** come. We're ready for them.' But neither he nor I had any idea how events would unfold within the next few hours. Nor did I know that before I would get home at 3.00 a.m. the feud would virtually be over.

Midnight was approaching fast, and our prayer walk teams were thinking more about home than about anything developing during those last moments. The night had been tense, but the streets were quiet when suddenly we heard screaming and shouting coming from 'Johnny's street'. The Lower Shankill had finally come under attack. What looked like a dozen or more cars drove into the neighbourhood and within moments the area was swamped with UDA men from other parts of the Shankill community, including those C/Company members who had jumped ship during the night.

They fought hand to hand with any of the C/Company men who still happened to be in the street at that time, who were there simply because they were under orders, and not because they wanted to fight. However, the 'main players' had received notice from a 'friendly caller' that an attack was imminent, which enabled them to escape just moments before the fighting began. Taking whatever they were able to carry, including substantial amounts of cash, they fled the area. They made their way to the boat and travelled during the midnight hours to Scotland and eventually on to England. They left their unsuspecting and ill-prepared 'foot soldiers', i.e. expendable pawns, to hold the fort.

At the time of the attack I had been sitting in someone's home within the Lower Shankill. I heard the screams of people in the street and immediately made my way to where the fighting had been taking place. Within a matter of minutes the fighting was over, but in the darkness I could see cars in the middle of the street, as if they had been abandoned. They were sitting where they had come to a halt; some with doors lying open, and some with the engine still running.

There were also several military and police vehicles sitting along the street, with dozens of heavily armed soldiers and police officers standing alongside. Then I noticed in the darkness that lined along one of the gable walls were about 20 men. Each one of these men had his hands raised in the air and a police officer standing in front of him, pointing a gun directly at his head.

As I walked into the middle of this scene, a scene that looked like a remake of a *Lethal Weapon* movie, I heard someone call out, 'Hey, Pastor Jack! Pastor Jack!' I immediately froze to the spot and the person continued to shout, 'You came to us for help last night and we've done you a favour. Can you do anything to help us?' Puzzled, I looked around, and there standing against the wall was one of the two men I had spoken to for 50 minutes the previous night.

Now I knew that these were members of a terrorist organization and that they were involved in a feud. I knew that I had often been vocal in my public condemnation of this group for various reasons. I also knew that this same organization had sentenced me to death on at least one occasion, which I wrote about in my previous book. And here were some of its men up against a wall and under arrest. Yet for some reason, and against my better judgement, I felt I needed to do something to help the situation move forward. So with a brass neck I asked to speak with the police officer in charge and soon found myself looking up into the eyes of what looked like Darth Vader.

My heartfelt feeling, as clearly expressed to the officer in charge, was that those men who were being stood against the wall were all members of the feuding organization, but that they had effectively dealt with what to them was an internal problem. No one had been killed or seriously injured. It seemed that the feud, particularly as it had affected the Lower Shankill, was over and that the arrest of those being held against the wall would serve no purpose.

'Darth' leaned over and asked, 'What is it you want me to do?' So I took a deep breath and said, 'Let them go!' He said, 'What?' So again I said in a loud whisper, 'Let them go!' He responded in kind by saying, 'I can't just let them go. There are other units here from different parts of the city, and there are soldiers present. I can't just let them go.' But no sooner had he said this that another police officer, standing next to him listening to our conversation, screamed the words, 'Gun, gun!'

Immediately on hearing this, 'Darth Vader' ran for cover behind one of his armoured vehicles, leaving me standing in the open and in the dark. He was immediately followed by every police officer and every soldier in the street! Left standing against the wall were the 20 men who had been arrested. With their hands still in the air they turned and looked at each other in total bewilderment, but realizing they were now on their own they ran for their cars, which were still sitting in front of them with doors open and engines running.

I could hardly believe what I was seeing. This was now looking more like a remake of *Police Academy* (not that I watch such nonsense), but it was really happening. I was still standing in the centre of the road trying to unravel in my mind the things I had seen with my eyes. I had not heard any gunfire, I had not seen any guns other than those being carried by the security forces, yet the police and soldiers were hiding!

The man who had earlier called out to me for help had also jumped into his car, but before driving away he stopped alongside me and said, 'Thanks, Jack! You can tell the people in the Lower Shankill it's all over. They've nothing to fear now. They've suffered long enough.' And with this he drove off.

The police and the soldiers then came out from behind their vehicles, but the men against the wall were all gone. Soon the police and the soldiers were also gone and within moments the streets were quiet. The immediate result of this was that the Lower Shankill was once again under the control of the mainline UDA, with a new brigadier put in Johnny Adair's place before the dust had even settled.

What this would mean for those living within the community remained to be seen in the coming weeks. The fact is that the whole situation was a disaster for everyone, whether it was those who had to leave Northern Ireland along with their families or those who remained behind to pick up the pieces, but most of all for those who had lost precious loved ones.

Although we believed this was effectively an end to the feud, we decided to continue with our prayer walk for the entire four weeks. The feud might well have come to an end on the third night of our prayer walk, but we knew this was not a time to slacken or to simply take our ease, for we understood that the very nature of evil would still be lurking and that we needed to continue to stand, walk and pray for the community and for all those affected by this tragic event. We also knew that the cross still needed to be lifted above the gun, and we were committed to doing so for however long it was necessary, but at least for the duration of the next three and a half weeks.

Although many were to remain fearful, and although there were those living within the Lower Shankill who did not trust the new UDA leadership, the fact is there was evidence during the coming weeks of a determination by the new leadership to improve the lot of those living within the Lower Shankill community, although most were only surface improvements. However, tragically, as we will see in a moment, not every promise they made was kept.

There is no doubt that during those weeks we had some God-given opportunities to pray with people and share testimonies of God's amazing grace. Many expressed their appreciation for our presence on the streets as we continued night after night to walk the streets and to talk and pray with those who were willing to converse with us. However, although there was a very definite improvement in the atmosphere of the community, there were still tensions. Some continued to leave the Lower Shankill, because they could not trust the new UDA leadership and were fearful of what might yet happen.

It brought home to us the reality that fighting and winning the battle in the heavenly places through prayer and intercession brings impacting results on the streets and in the community. We witnessed some of the external/surface changes taking place, as seen in the following: some of the more offensive terrorist murals and other trappings on the sides of people's homes were removed; 18 pipe-bombs were dropped off on a waste ground and were discovered by the police thanks to a 'friendly' phone call; some of the older members of the UDA were allowed to leave the organization and others were sent home after being told they would no longer need to attend weekly meetings or to keep guard at certain homes. The UDA also announced that their organization had begun a year of military inactivity. Sounded good, but time would tell!

All of the above had taken place within the first three weeks of our four-week prayer walk. The one thing that was noticeable to all our teams during those weeks was the amazing sense of calm within the Lower Shankill community and the removal of much of the terrorist paraphernalia. Compared to what it was like four weeks previously, this was nothing short of miraculous.

However, we were not foolish enough to think that the terrorist machine had gone away. It had not, and still has not! Nor have they kept all the promises they made to the people in the Lower Shankill, particularly promises given to Alan McCullough. He tragically accepted assurances regarding his safety from the leadership of the UDA, but their word meant nothing. Alan was lured to his death, and his gunshot body was finally found in a ditch one week after he was murdered.

Alan was the son of William (Bucky) McCullough, who had been murdered by the INLA in 1981. I wrote an account of Bucky's murder in my previous book *Through Terror and Adversity*. I never thought when I began writing this book that I would be including an account of the murder of Bucky's youngest son. Our thoughts and prayers go out to Barbara who, having gone through the trauma of losing her husband has once again known the grief of such loss, only this time the loss of a son. Our thoughts and prayers also go out to his surviving brother Kenny and his sisters who all experienced the loss of a father and now more recently the loss of a brother. And of course our thoughts and prayers go out to all those who have suffered during the recent years of violence that has plagued our beloved Northern Ireland, particularly to those families who lost loved ones during this UFF feud.

The ongoing challenge

Cleaning up the image is one thing, but dealing with the core issues such as violence, drugs and crime etc, is another thing entirely. In doing our part we helped to win the initial battle through prayer and through physical presence within the streets. We did what we could to lift the cross above the gun, whether it was through the Cross Walk or through the Prayer Walk, and as a church, no matter what others might think or say about us or whatever the danger to ourselves, we will continue to respond to whatever challenge is placed before us by God.

The roaring lion that seeks to devour might still well be out there and will always recruit its allies, but the cross will still be lifted above the gun by those who are allied to One who is always victorious. We are not simply on the winning side, but are on the side that has won. See for yourself – Read the end of the world's 'Best Seller'. It's called 'The Bible'.

For further information, please feel free to write to:
New Life Ministries Ireland
134a Shankill Road
Belfast BT13 1FT

For those living in the USA, please feel free to write to:
New Life Ministries Ireland
C/o The McInerneys
15370 Secret Hollow Place
Waldorf MD 20601

Email: jack.mckee1@btinternet.com
Website: www.newlifeministriesireland.co.uk